THE MODERN COCKTAIL

First published in 2017 by
Jacqui Small
An imprint of Quarto Publishing PLC
74–77 White Lion Street
London N1 9PF

Publisher: Jacqui Small
Commissioning Editor/Project Editor: Joanna Copestick
Managing Editor: Emma Heyworth-Dunn
Senior Designer: Rachel Cross
Photography: Richard Jung
Production: Maeve Healy

Co-writer: Imogen Fortes

ISBN: 978 1 911127 23 9

A catalogue record for this book is available
from the British Library.

2019 2018 2017
10 9 8 7 6 5 4 3 2 1

Printed in China

MIX
Paper from
responsible sources
FSC® C008047

THE MODERN COCKTAIL

FLAVOUR + INNOVATION

TALENTED MR FOX

MATT WHILEY

'People who don't like cocktails like Matt's drinks and people who don't like bartenders like Matt. He is creative, intelligent and driven and it's those qualities that make him the best in the country.'

Michael O'Hare, The Man Behind The Curtain

jacqui small

CONTENTS

INTRODUCTION

I fell into being a bartender. I left school when I was 16 and the only academic thing I'd cared about was my sport GCSE. As a youngster, I simply wanted to play sport. I was in the junior ranks of the England cricket squad, progressing well, then at the age of 24 I injured myself pretty seriously.

The transition to bartending was nothing more than a series of coincidences. I was in a bar one night with a friend whose mate was the manager and they needed some help for a private party. I was really useless – copying the guys I was working with, holding the bottles weirdly – but I loved it. I enjoyed the interaction with people; the buzz, the pace. A second opportunity to help came up the next night and things just went from there. Being a sportsman means I'm competitive, so I immediately wanted to get good at the job. I wanted knowledge – how to make the drinks and interact with guests. There's a way of interacting with people so that you can work, but still mix great cocktails. I got advice from people I thought were good and within a year I was managing the bar.

After moving to London I was asked to join the restaurant Zuma as the bartender and I jumped at the chance. The environment in a high-end restaurant bar is very different to an independent bar. It's focused – the aim is to be brilliant. You're there to work hard and to look after people rather than party with them. That experience was a defining moment for me. The bar was busy and the job was stressful, but it changed me, changed my attitude and gave me an understanding and a respect for the profession that has endured.

Fast forward a few years and I co-founded a drinks company – bringing creative cocktails to events. This flowed into consultancy work and then naturally led into the idea of setting up a bar. London's Marylebone became the backdrop for Purl, which opened in May 2010.

At the time Purl was pretty revolutionary. It pioneered the way in bringing the behind-the-scenes style of cocktail making to customers (previously that really serious kind of cocktail making had been confined to competitions). Purl was an opportunity to bring something new and very customer-focused to the drinks scene – a theatrical and multi-sensory style of drink made with flair, and I think we achieved that. People have gone on to recreate our ideas and I take a lot of pride in that. When I started I looked at bartenders from the 1800s and recreated

their drinks – it's an industry where recycling is inevitable. Just because you change a drop of bitters, it doesn't mean you've created a new drink. The foundations of what we do were built by bartenders over 100 years ago, so heritage is something to be admired and learned from.

Worship Street Whistling Shop, a Dickensian low-key venue, followed Purl's success in 2011 before I decided to launch my own company – a pop-up called Talented Mr Fox – set within a boutique London hotel. It later became the permanent bar until the hotel was sold. In 2014 I opened the Peg + Patriot at the Town Hall Hotel in Bethnal Green. The area of Bethnal Green has changed since we opened and so has the bar – above all, the style of drinks has evolved. At the start I was well aware that we'd been very experimental with Talented Mr Fox. I still wanted to have very experimental drinks on the bar, but I also wanted to ease into it. We didn't have massive footfall; people need to travel to Bethnal Green, so I wanted to make sure there were elements to the drinks that were recognizable and understandable, so we didn't put people off before they'd got through the door. Now there are more bars in the area and people understand what we do, so we've been able to go back to doing what we want to – working with flavours and making drinks that are exciting and tasty. I've always just wanted to innovate, to be different and creative – at the forefront of change.

How my bars are run and the people I work with are also very important to me. I want everyone to be as excited about what we serve and create as I am – they all need to be able to talk passionately about the drinks and sell them to guests, otherwise it's not convincing. So we create the menu as a team – even the least experienced person in the bar. We all come up with ideas, then make the drinks together. I will tweak them and suggest how I think they can be made better, then everyone goes away and refines them. It's an evolving process. Of course we need to balance the style of drink we offer across the whole menu – long, short, strong, sweet etc. – but nothing makes the menu until everyone's happy with it. That's just the way I work.

If something's not selling we don't change it. If we believe it's good we don't take it off the menu. Not every drink needs to be a bestseller; even if someone only buys that drink occasionally, it means there's a drink for them. The aim of the game is simple: it's for people to walk out of the door happier than when they arrived, and to have paid for something they've really enjoyed.

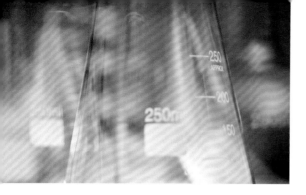

BARTENDING

INNOVATION + EVOLUTION

Although as an industry, bartending is inextricably linked to the restaurant world, until recently the making and crafting of drinks has worked in a very different way. Drinks industry icons might not be as famous as the household-name chefs (yet…), but the two industries and the ideas behind their primary role – to serve up a great gustatory experience – are becoming more in sync, as drinks customers are starting to be more discerning and bartenders look to restaurants to learn about flavour and ingredients.

One of the questions I'm most often asked about opening a bar or making cocktails is who or what influences me, and the simple answer is, chefs. Certain chefs inspire me for different reasons, but I am always influenced by the way they work with produce and the respect they have for it. I'm a big admirer of Heston Blumenthal for his pioneering work and his creativity; Magnus Nilsson of Fäviken for the way he uses ingredients; Massimo Bottura of Osteria Francescana, for his spirit, his exuberance and the way he interacts with guests; New York's Wylie Dufresne for his innovation at wd-50 and Alder; and finally Tom Sellers of Restaurant Story in London, with whom I work closely, and who has a similar mentality to Heston – he draws a lot of inspiration from his childhood.

I'm always going into chef's kitchens when I can – to listen and learn and watch the way they work with their ingredients and with flavours. It's something that never fails to inspire me. And bartenders generally have started to think a bit more like chefs and to treat the components in their recipes in a similar way. Where previously we bought in liqueurs and syrups, now we make things to our own specification, with produce we can buy and tailor to our flavour requirements for really creative bespoke drinks. It's an exciting time for the industry.

Scout bar, London.

THE DEVELOPMENT OF THE COCKTAIL

It's well documented that mixed drinks have been around since at least the 1700s – punch came to the UK from India via sailors from the British East India Company (the Sanskrit word 'panch', meaning 'five', represents the five elements of the drink: alcohol; water; sugar; citrus and spice) – the 'cocktail' officially came much later. Its exact origins are still debated, but it is fairly widely recognized that the first mention of the term appeared in a newspaper in Vermont in 1803, while the man often described as the father of bartending, 'Professor' Jerry Thomas, wrote the world's first book containing cocktail recipes *The Bartender's Guide: How to Mix Drinks* in 1862.

The industry has come a long way since then: styles of bar, the role of a bartender and fashions in drinks have all changed, of course, but the biggest change over the last 10 to 15 years has been for bartenders to revisit the cocktail's history and to comb the past for classic recipes and mixing techniques. My own view is that the classics are interesting (I wouldn't have a job without them); they give you a guideline and a grounding, in the same way that many good chefs have undergone classical culinary training to understand fundamental principles. And throughout the process of constructing a drink I will always think about how closely it is linked to a classic – I'll notice if it's in the daiquiri style, for example, but I don't think that just because a drink stems from a classic recipe that it's necessarily the right recipe for right now. Palates have changed and many of the original recipes are way too sweet for a modern palate. I like to take the classic recipe as a basis and then challenge it. So if someone comes to the bar and orders an old fashioned or any other established drink, we offer a version of every single one, but they're made in a way that we think tastes good. It's not about being provocative or rebellious, it's about playing with flavours and always striving for the best.

As people have become more interested in food and we've witnessed the rise of the 'foodie', they've also become interested in new flavours and their palates have become more discerning. It follows that the same desire for experimentation and openness has been reflected in the drinks they're choosing. Whereas previously it would have been fairly inconceivable for a menu to have a whole section

Earth + Trees, a twist on the classic martini at Rök Smokehouse in London.

Parsnip, a cocktail from Scout, garnished with nettles.

devoted to savoury cocktails, now it's something that intrigues and appeals to – guests' palates. In some ways this means that, as bartenders, we have an easier job; drinkers are willing to try new things, but it also means we've had to adapt and change, and move with these mutating trends and tastes. One of the biggest developments has been that bartenders, like chefs, have started to think seasonally. The way I run my bars is ultra seasonal – one of my producers only stocks ingredients that are in season; and I also buy from a forager.

FORAGED INGREDIENTS

Chefs often use foraged ingredients so they're something I became interested in learning more about before I started to use them in my drinks. Using this type of ingredient is something I'm now passionate about – there is so much produce in our wilderness just sitting there – in our hedgerows, marshlands, coastlands and forests – while we continue to mass-farm fruit from other countries or buy it in. Often it isn't fresh and not that tasty. Working with a forager provides me with a whole new range of flavours and ingredients to play and work with. What's more it's not only more sustainable, it's stimulating and pushes all of us at the bars to be more creative. A bellini on the menu at one of the restaurants I consult for changes regularly according to what seasonal produce has been provided to us by our forager.

With all this has also come an awareness of the need to reduce our waste and improve sustainability within the industry. I buy a lot of class 2 fruit, for example – fruit that's going off – partly for cost reasons, but partly because, if I'm going to ferment it, the sugars have already started to break down. We ferment fruit to change their flavour, to reduce sugar levels, add acidity and carbonation and to bring out the vinegar notes – we stop it at different times and to get different products – so it makes real economic sense to use fruit that are part of the way there. And as with everything I do, it's interesting. If you've got strawberries going out of season, for example, it gives you the opportunity to preserve them.

One of the other most recent developments in the industry, and perhaps one of the most surprising, is the rise of the 'mocktail' (a cocktail without any alcohol). Rather than being an afterthought (at best, just an ill-considered mixture of whatever juices and soft drinks happen to be behind the bar that day), bars are waking up to the fact that more and more people aren't drinking alcohol, so mocktails are starting to assume greater prominence on menus. I always have a mocktail section on mine. There shouldn't be a taboo about people not wanting to drink, and I want customers to feel that they're part of the same experience, so I make drinks that reflect this: we've had non-alcoholic Campari and soda, gin and tonic, and a piña colada soda on the menu.

LESS LIQUOR, LESS SUGAR

In a similar vein the movement towards eating less sugar is a strong one. Until recently there was no real awareness of how much hidden sugar there is in cocktails. For a while I've been making a conscious effort to reduce the quantity of sugar in my drinks. I use sugar as a mouthfeel – adding a maximum of 5ml (1tsp) sugar to each cocktail, where most bartenders would use 15–20ml (3–4tsp). In citrus drinks, for example, sugar is often used to offset the sourness from the lemon but I'd simply use less citrus to begin with; that way you need less sugar. The drink will still have a very zesty aroma and you'll taste more of the base spirit.

Sea buckthorn is a versatile marshland ingredient.

THE BAR, THE VIBE

If someone could bottle the ingredients that make up a good bar, they'd make a fortune. Sadly it's really not that simple. A good bar has 'vibe' – essentially, atmosphere and the right mood – and as a bar owner or manager that's simply something that you've got to create yourself; there's no definitive answer.

Above all you create it with people – no good bar is empty, of course – but there are a few factors that I consider essential in making a bar feel welcoming and leaving your guests wanting to return. For me this starts with great staff. They've got to be good at what they do; passionate about what they make; and above all good communicators so that they can relay that passion to their guests.

Good lighting is key to making people feel comfortable and setting a tone; and you need the right sound. Not necessarily the music; although music does create mood; it's the level of noise in the room that creates the right atmosphere. Too loud and you can't communicate; too quiet and you feel you have to whisper.

A good product is what makes people come back. Your location helps but it's not essential. If you open a good bar anywhere, it will succeed (provided you're paying the right rent), but a good location with plenty of footfall does of course help get people through the door.

Finally, you need to understand who you want in. If you want to be a party bar – you decide on your product and lay the bar out in a certain way. If you want to give people an experience, then your product and the mood you create are going to be different. At the Peg, I simply wanted people who were open to new ideas and wanted to try something new. Age isn't important – it's about mentality.

The rest is up to you – the materials and furnishing, the design, the size of the room. Textures are important to me, so at the Peg I didn't want the walls to have a smooth finish (they have a coarse, pitted feel to them). Even if you can't see it or even notice it, I believe it gives depth to the bar and a feeling without guests really realizing. I also wanted the bar to feel like you were in Bethnal Green so there are elements that aren't necessarily finished – just a simple nod to the area, which is still changing and evolving. I also happen to like small bars – you can be selective with what you do and you don't need to have such wide appeal

FLAVOUR

UNDERSTANDING FLAVOUR

Since becoming a bartender my palate has evolved; or at least I understand flavour more – I understand what I'm looking for. A lot of people will tell you they don't have a 'good palate', but in reality almost everybody has a sense of taste. Having a good palate or not is just a question of understanding what to look for when you taste something; understanding and knowing what is bitter and why; or what is salty, sweet or sour. A lot of people who drink in bars mistake sour with bitter, for example, but there's a clear distinction. As a bartender you need to be able to understand the different aspects of flavour to be able to adjust them in drinks, but also to be able to explain them to customers.

All over the world there are bars pushing the boundaries with flavour and getting more and more experimental, being bolder and more outlandish with their combinations. This proves that there's an appetite and a curiosity among customers to try new things. That said, there are still a lot of people who don't like stepping out of their comfort zone and are sceptical of anything out of the ordinary. While of course I'm more interested in getting people to try things, there's definitely a place for both scenarios to cohabit. And for anybody who is on the fence or nervous about trying different flavours, what I would encourage them to do is to talk to the bartender. If they're unsure about choosing a drink or want to know more – start a conversation; get the information about that drink and then decide whether to give it a go or not.

THE FIVE TYPES OF FLAVOUR

Our tongues can discern five basic tastes: sweet, salty, sour, bitter and umami. Flavour, however, combines taste and smell: we register flavour through our nose almost as much as our tongue, which is why if you have a cold and your nose is blocked, you won't be able to taste well. The tastes our tongue senses are roughly defined as follows:

From left to right, top to bottom: Sourness/limes; bitterness/chicory; umami/Marmite malt extract; sweetness/pineapple; saltiness/rock salt.

✳ SOURNESS

Anything where one of the main components is acidic; in drinks it will predominantly come from citrus fruit – e.g. lime, lemon, yuzu – and vinegar, as well as powdered acids, such as citric or malic acid.

☕ BITTERNESS

A human's most sensitive taste, mainly because evolution has trained us to believe that anything bitter is toxic or harmful to us.

🌿 SAVOURY (SALTINESS)

Anything that contains sodium chloride, or other salts. Most foods aren't naturally salty – they contain sodium but not necessarily big quantities of sodium chloride – so we add salt.

An example of a natural salty flavour (rather than umami flavour, see right) in a drink would be seaweed or sea greens. However, for the purposes of classifying drinks in the table on page 32, I've taken a 'salty' taste and used the wider term 'savoury' to describe drinks as anything that isn't sweet, bitter, spicy or specifically umami.

⬡ SWEETNESS

Defined by the presence of sugars. Sugar was once a dominant component in cocktails, but as palates have changed and more people are thinking about health and well-being, the trend for very sweet drinks and using lots of sugar in cocktails has been declining. It doesn't mean that sugar will disappear from drinks completely – sweet flavours are needed for balancing the five flavours – but there will be a greater reliance on healthier natural sugars, such as fruit.

🍄 UMAMI

A Japanese word, literally meaning 'good flavour'. Umami foods are characterized as containing glutamates, a type of amino acid, and in English the taste is best described as 'savoury' or 'meaty'. While this could be confusing, in that it's quite close to saltiness, umami foods are most commonly meat-based, seafood-based or well fermented, such as cheese (Parmigiano is the strongest in umami), and cured (Parma ham, bacon, salamis etc.). Tinned anchovies, Marmite, oyster sauce, tomatoes and mushrooms are other examples of food high in umami, and in drinks, ale, wine and black tea are the highest.

Other theories will argue that taste can be categorized further but these five are a good means of defining and categorizing a drink.

When it comes to using these tastes when I construct a drink, I will decide at the start what sort of drink I'm going to make – you're not going to be able to fit all five tastes into a drink but certain tastes work well together. Umami goes quite well with sour, for example, and you can't use sour alone – it needs to be balanced with sweetness. My bar teams and I really like umami, for example, but we have to remember that not everybody is as accustomed to finding these kinds of savoury ingredients in drinks, so we need to balance the umami with other tastes and often dial it back. The tastes have to talk to each other and work together without one dominating.

We also need to think about how the tastes work across a whole drink. So many times, I've tried a drink and thought I didn't like it, then three sips later, I'll think it's awesome. You've got to go back to something and try it again. It's like wine – sommeliers will often tell you to take a second sip of a wine before deciding whether you like it or not because your palate becomes receptive to something the more you try it. And finally a drink changes as it gets warm. In the same way that the flavour of your coffee changes as it cools (try it), the temperature of your cocktail, as well as how much any ice has melted, affects the taste.

CONSTRUCTING COCKTAILS

In the same way that chefs are the people who inspire me, the way I create my drinks comes from food. When I'm making a new drink, I'll often think about a dish that I've had recently or a food I like, and see if there's a way of turning it into a liquid form. It's why our drinks list at the bars often read like a restaurant menu – we've had everything from black pudding- and cauliflower-inspired drinks to Monster Munch and jam tart cocktails.

But after I've created the main flavour by making a distillate of it (see page 214 for more about distillates), the next element to focus on is the base and how I'm going to use and build that flavour around it. The base is the main alcohol, which is generally a spirit, but it could also be a wine, sparkling wine or sake. I'll try combining the distillate with a variety of different spirits to establish which works best. Generally I know whether it's going to suit a dark or a clear spirit and I have a good idea of what's going to taste good, but sometimes I'll be surprised.

The next element to consider when you're constructing a drink is whether you want it long or short, and in the case of short drinks whether it's going to be served straight up or over ice.

A **LONG** cocktail is anything that is low ABV (6–14%) and served in a highball. Long drinks are generally lengthened with something with bubbles: tonic water, sparkling wine etc., although it could also be flat; we've used coconut water, for example. The use of carbonation means that long drinks are generally best made with light spirits; if you mix whisky with carbonation, for example, the wood in the whisky can come through as bitter and tannic. It's not to say dark spirits won't work; it's just less common an approach.

Long cocktails are characterized by being easy to drink; they're more approachable for many casual cocktail drinkers, particularly for people who don't want a strong hit of alcohol.

A **SHORT** cocktail is anything that's around 20% ABV. They're served either straight up, which means they'll have been shaken or stirred in a shaker then poured directly into a martini-style glass, or over ice in a rocks glass. As a general rule, short drinks on the rocks work better made with dark spirits; straight up work with either.

Long Cocktail – Woodford Remake.   *Short Cocktail – Whisky Sour.*

CATEGORIZING COCKTAILS

TASTE AND FLAVOUR

There's no perfect formula for how to categorize cocktails, and of course every bartender will have a different method. For the purposes of this book and to help you work out what you like, I've created a table that 'classifies' the drinks in this book according to certain criteria (see page 32). It's based around the questions I'd ask you if you were making a drink for you. I'd start with the type of spirit you like; then ascertain taste preference – sweet, sour, umami etc.; whether you like long or short drinks (and then whether you wanted it straight up or over ice); and finally I'd try and narrow the choice a little by ascertaining if you like a certain 'subcategory' of drink: minerality, herbaceousness, dryness, smokiness etc.

DRY

Dryness is something that is quite hard to define. In cocktails it's predominantly used within the context of a martini, as a means of specifying the type of martini you want, but it's also used heavily in wine and beer descriptions. In wine, it refers to the level of sweetness or residual sugar in a wine. A wine is considered 'dry' when all of the grape sugar is converted to alcohol during fermentation, while a sweet wine will have some residual sugar. The term can get confusing though, because sensitivity to sweetness varies from person to person, and because sometimes a wine will technically be dry but give the impression of being sweet because the grapes were very ripe or the oak barrels imparted a sense of sweetness to the wine.

In terms of a cocktail, the principle is the same, dry cocktails have nearly no sweetness and therefore dry is a categorisation that is quite rare, principally applied to martinis and Manhattans. A martini for example has a little bit of sweetness from the vermouth, but the sensation in your mouth is as if there were no sweetness as it's balanced by the acidity that comes from the botanicals too. It's also why a martini is the only drink that doesn't fit into any taste categorisation – the sweetness is so marginal that you can't describe the drink as sweet, yet neither does it match any of the other taste profiles.

As an aside, there is some confusion over what is meant by a 'dry' martini. To clarify, a dry martini isn't a martini made without vermouth (all martinis have vermouth unless you ask for an

Perfect Martini.

'extra dry, or bone dry martini' where it will be as little as the glass being rinsed in vermouth, or even none at all), it's a martini with dry gin and dry vermouth and the dryness refers to the quantity used in the drink. The drier the martini, the less vermouth is added.

HERBACEOUS

Anything that when you taste or smell it has the characteristics of a peppery, spicy, herb such as coriander (cilantro) or rocket (arugula). Even though tequila doesn't contain any herbs, I would describe it as herbaceous as it has a definite spicy herb aroma.

MINERALITY

This generally comes from an ingredient's origins: in wine it will come from the soil; in whisky from the peat; seaweed from the sea. It tastes earthy or when you drink it you can taste a mineral, as if you were drinking a mineral water with a high mineral content – or licking a rock! I've distilled rocks, oyster shells, seaweed, soil even, to achieve minerality.

FRUITY

Anything where the forward flavour of the drink is fruit – berries, apples etc. – it doesn't have to be the main ingredient; it can simply be the strongest flavour to come through.

SMOKY

Anything that has a burnt or smoked flavour. Sometimes this will come from the spirit –

a whisky or a mezcal are both very smoky; however, sometimes I'll impart the flavour myself, say if I've smoked a fruit or burnt an ingredient (see also page 201).

NUTTY

A drink with a seed or nut content; we'll generally achieve this by distilling a nut or seed with a spirit.

AROMATIC/SPICY

Anything that is heavily spiced.

RICH

Essentially this denotes viscosity and something that has low acidity. It can come from different forms: cream, coconut, banana or egg white.

FRESH

Something that tastes like it's just been picked, or that contains a crisp, cooling ingredient such as watermelon or cucumber.

FLORAL

Anything that uses flowers – elderflowers, violets etc. – and where that flavour is the most dominant.

CLASSIFYING COCKTAILS

✻ SOUR   ⊗ BITTER   ⚘ SAVOURY   ⬢ SWEET   🍄 UMAMI

SPIRIT	COCKTAIL NAME	FLAVOUR	SUB FLAVOUR	LONG/ SHORT
GIN	BURNT FOOL (p.90)	✻ Sour	Fruity	Long
	THE COLOUR BLUE (p.92)	✻ Sour	Minerally	Long
	PEG LONDON DRY G&T (p.88)	⊗ Bitter/Sweet	Herbaceous	Long
	STORY MARTINI (p.100)	⬢ ⊗ Sweet/Sour	Fruity/Herbaceous	Short
	MONSTER MUNCH GIBSON (p.94)	⚘ Savoury	Dry	Short
	RÖK HOUSE BELLINI (p.98)	⚘ ✻ Savoury/ Sour	Herbaceous	Long
	BASTARDIZED GIN MARTINI (p.102)	None	Minerally	Short
VODKA	APPLE (p.118)	✻ Sour	Floral	Long
	CARROT (p.128)	✻ Sour	Earthy	Short
	TMF BLOODY MARY (p.116)	✻ 🍄 Sour/Umami	Spicy	Long
	RHUBARB (p.136)	✻ ⊗ Sour/Sweet	Fresh/Piney	Long
	EARTH & TREES (p.124)	⚘ Savoury	Dry, Smoky, Minerally	Short
	BOTTLE #1 TOMATO (p.126)	⚘ Savoury	Aromatic	Long
	BANGKOK PENICILLIN (p.108)	⚘ ✻ Savoury/Sour	Spicy	Short
	VIET SALAD (p.120)	⚘ ✻ Savoury/Sour	Nutty	Short
	BELLINI (RABBIT) (p.134)	⚘ ⬢ Savoury/ Sweet	Toasted	Long
	MI-SO HAPPY (p.106)	🍄 ✻ Umami/Sour	Fruity	Long
	CHERRY BARK (p.132)	⬢ Sweet	Spicy/Perfumed	Short
	PERFECT MARTINI (p.112)	None	Dry/Herbaceous	Short

SPIRIT	COCKTAIL NAME	FLAVOUR	SUB FLAVOUR	LONG/ SHORT
WHISKY + BOURBON	WOODFORD REMAKE (p.144)	🌸 Sour	Dry/Fruity	Short
	WHISKY SOUR (p.154)	🌸 Sour	Aromatic	Short
	E2PA (p.142)	🧊 Sweet	Rich	Long
	METAL MAN (p.148)	🧊 Sweet	Dry/Rich	Short
	SUPER SOAKER (p.150)	🧊 Sweet	Fresh	Short
	PARSNIP (p.152)	🧊 Sweet	Rich	Short
WINE + VERMOUTH	THOMAS WOLSEY (p.168)	🌸 Sour	Fruity	Long
	FORAGED NEGRONI (p.174)	🌿 Bitter	Floral	Short
	PEA WINE (p.160)	🌾 Savoury	Dry/Herbaceous	Long
	SMOKED PEACH BELLINI (p.166)	🌾 🧊 Savoury/ Sweet	Smoky	Long
	BIRDS (p.170)	🌾 🧊 Savoury/ Sweet-ish	Aromatic/Milk/ Citrus	Short
	BLACKBERRY PINE (p.164)	None	Dry	Long
OTHER DRINKS				
RUM	PEANUT COLADA (p.178)	🌸 Sour	Rich	Long
	SCALLOP PAIRING (p.180)	🌸 Sour	Fresh	Short
TEQUILA	MARGARITA (p.182)	🌸 Sour	Fresh/Minerally	Short
	LACK OF FAITH (p.184)	🌾 Savoury	Dry/Smoky	Short
COGNAC	GRONER SAZERAC (p.186)	🌾 Savoury	Dry	Short
	PRETZEL MANGER (p.188)	🌾 Savoury	Nutty/Dry	Short
RAKI	TURKISH COFFEE (p.190)	🥤 Umami	Aromatic	Short
SAKE	BOTTLE #3 RICE (p.194)	🌸 Sour	Aromatic	Long
	BOTTLE #2 BANANA (p.193)	🌾 🧊 Savoury/ Sweet	Fresh	Long

SPIRITS

CHOOSING + USING

Selecting spirits is a matter of taste, opinion, preference and palate – these are what will determine your choices. There is a reason why there are hundreds of gins on the market – it's because people are looking to keep tasting different things. Of course, at home you're not going to have a selection of each spirit to choose from – even we don't here; we only have two vodkas, for example – so all I can advise about choosing your spirits is to keep trying different products to work out what you like. Of course, you can get quite a good range of decent spirits in the supermarket, but I would recommend buying at specialist spirit shops. Not only will you get a wider selection, but additionally the staff will be knowledgeable and be able to advise you. They'll know the distilleries and makers of the products and will be able to recommend how you get the best quality of bottle for your budget. And above all, they'll be able to help you ascertain what you might like. Alternatively, on page 220 I've listed some of the best online stockists for spirits; they've all got tasting notes so that you can make an informed decision about what you're buying.

Another great way to choose spirits is to try before you buy by ordering samples. Master of Malt (see page 220 for details) sells small 'taster' bottles that you can order to have a small taste of a spirit before you invest in the large bottles.

I know there's a lot of choice out there so the easiest thing to do at home is just to pick something. Start somewhere. If it's gin, read the list of ingredients – look at what botanicals are in it. If there's a flavour you particularly like then go for that one.

On the following pages are a guide to the main spirits and fortified wines I use to make my cocktails and how I go about choosing a brand and why. My aim is that it will help you when you're weighing up what to look for in the spirits you choose, but it is by no means a list of the ones I think you should buy – as ever, that is down to your preferences.

GIN

Although it's been around for centuries, gin has had a real resurgence in the past few years and there has been an explosion of 'craft gins' (gins made by small-batch artisan distillers) coming on to the UK market. Gin appeared in the UK thanks to the Dutch, but we embraced it warmly – and today the British love of mother's milk (or mother's ruin, depending on how you choose to look at it) is just as enthusiastic; and a gin and tonic remains one of our most requested drinks. At my bars we've also been a part of the craft gin revolution and make three gins ourselves. Gin is actually quite easy to distill once you understand the process and the ratio of what needs to go into it, and we wanted to make our own to experiment with different botanicals and the versatility of the spirit, but above all to be able to create the flavours we needed for our drinks.

We make a London Dry gin on site; a seasonal gin, where the ingredients change depending on what produce is available – it's based on rosemary and sea fennel in the winter for example, and in the summer on fruits such as raspberries, strawberries and rosehips. We also make a gin that's specifically for martinis, which is heavily citrussed. Plus, we have a gin that we sell to other bars but it's now distilled for us off site. It's quite an unusual one – a gin made from hops and without any citrus, which was an idea fuelled by the craft beer movement. It's an unusual flavour, and for the bars that stock it it's a novel way of offering something a bit quirky and different to their customers.

A London Dry gin is generally a good choice for use in cocktails as it mixes well with other flavours. Our London Dry is designed to work in everything. By definition a London Dry must have a minimum of 37.5% ABV, contain no artificial ingredients and only a very small amount of sweetener. Of course, as with all gins, the dominant flavour needs to be the juniper berries, but there are no other flavour specifications, nor does it have to be made in London. The term 'London Dry' simply determines how it's made as you can't add any flavours after the distillation. Ours is quite citrussy, as we use both orange and lemon peel, but it also has a nice spicy backbone, which comes from liquorice and cinnamon; while dried orris root (the root of the iris flower) gives it a floral note.

Our seasonal gin is designed for making gin and tonics so we make sure it always has enough flavour and backbone that it can be diluted by the tonic. At Peg + Patriot we don't stock any mainstream brands; in addition to ours we have three others but they're from small craft distillers.

In some ways new generation gins are becoming more and more complex in flavour. Artisan makers are tending to use even more botanicals, herbs and spices for flavour and interest, stretching the boundaries of the flavour profile of gins and crafting them so they are best enjoyed neat, or simply with tonic.

I know there's a lot of choice out there so while for the bar my decisions are based on relationships and stories, the easiest thing to do at home is just to pick one. Most gins will work well in gin and tonics. If you don't have the budget to explore different kinds or are unsure about which flavour profiles you might like or will work in cocktails, go for Tanqueray, Beefeater or Bombay Sapphire. If you want to go for an artisan gin that is quite readily available, go for Fords, which is designed for cocktails.

VODKA

At Peg + Patriot we only stock two vodkas – as spirits go, vodkas are quite neutral in terms of their flavour profile, so although the two I have both have very different flavours, overall vodka doesn't range vastly so I don't feel the need to stock any more. Both our vodkas are made with winter wheat; the difference is that Konik's Tail has a spelt and a rye content, while Aylesbury Duck is purely the wheat. And from a taste perspective Konik's Tail is smooth with a light vanilla hint, whereas Aylesbury Duck has a caramelly note that I love.

There are, of course, a huge number of vodkas out there, so why these two? The reason is the same as for a lot of my choices, it's based on the relationship I have with the producer, somebody likeminded, and their story. I like using a brand where you get to speak to the people who make it. I met Pleurat Shabani, the London bartender who set up Konik's Tail, and loved his ethos and his integrity: he camped on farms to figure out when was the best time to pick his winter wheat and spelt. I tried his vodka and thought it was amazing; it worked in all the cocktails in which we tried it, as well as being a great vodka to drink neat, and I wanted to be part of his story.

The 86 Co., who created Aylesbury Duck vodka, was started by a group of bartenders from America who wanted to produce spirits designed for bartenders. I tried the range and loved it so that was it.

Vodka's neutral flavour profile means that it's a good and therefore popular base for cocktails. Most other spirits have strong flavours of their own, which can fight against the flavours you're trying to impart into a drink, while vodka is a fairly blank canvas. It also means that it's a good base for distillations (see page 214), as again it marries with other flavours easily.

WHISKY + BOURBON

Bourbon and rye whiskeys are my drink of choice so this is the biggest selection of any spirit I have at the bar. Bourbons are typically made in the southern states of America and for a whiskey to be considered bourbon the grain content must be at least 51 per cent corn, and the remainder different proportions of malted barley, rye and wheat. A 'rye' must be distilled from 51 per cent rye (that's in the US; in Canada it doesn't need to contain any at all). Bourbon can range in flavour, from being heavily corn-based to those that have a cinnamon or a caramel bias. Ryes are much more spicy.

I like to try new things all the time so I'm forever ordering in the products from new, small independent producers.

Which whisky to choose in a cocktail depends on the type of cocktail you're making. If you're looking for a sweeter outcome, go for bourbon as it has a natural sweetness. Rye is spicier, therefore it's generally drier so it gives a punchier flavour in a mixed drink. For cocktails, blended whiskies generally work best, largely on the basis that if you've got a single malt that's been carefully aged for 18 years you wouldn't really want to add anything to it, but perhaps that's just my view. As with everything you can use what you like, but I would generally advise sticking with a young or blended whisky.There are also fantastic whiskies from Japan as well as some great products coming out of Taiwan.

We have a lot of Scotch too; you have to because it's so diverse. Even within Scotland, it varies enormously between the regions. Despite coming from one grain, a single malt from each region will taste very different because the way they are made varies hugely according to the distiller. At the bar, we have whiskies that cover various taste profiles.

Blending whisky is such an art – the age to use each of the whiskies being blended and how to combine them is such a skill, and what the Scottish distilleries do is really amazing in terms of making unique products. I generally buy blended whiskies from Compass Box as every one I've tried has been amazing.

We also have five whiskies we decant so that they're in unlabelled, unbranded bottles. We label them sweet shop; waxy; minerally; chewy; and medicinal. It's purely so that people have a different way of picking a whisky. Rather than choosing an Islay because they know it's smoky, they're prompted to think about the type of smokiness they want. So both the minerally and the medicinal ones are in fact smoky, but they taste very different. The chewy one always intrigues people. It's a bold, thick whisky that feels like you've got to chew it a little. Such labelling gives people a different way to think about their drink.

RUM

Given that rum is made by fermenting sugar cane, it's no surprise that rum is one of the most naturally sweet spirits available to use in cocktails, although of the two main types – white and dark, white rums are much lighter and less sweet. White rums are fermented in steel canisters then filtered, while dark rum is aged for much longer in oak casks, giving a deep brown colour and a richer, more pronounced caramel flavour. In both cases, however, the rum available to buy today is changing in line with the fact that our palates are demanding less sugar. For example, the brand that I work with most often – Diplomatico – have just altered their blanco, raising the ABV from 40 to 47%, which makes it drier and therefore less sweet. They've also just released a dark rum called Mantuano and again, for a dark rum, it's much less sweet than its counterparts.

I use Diplomatico's blanco a lot in my cocktail recipes; it has been aged for six years which is a much longer maturation period than white rums are generally laid down for, meaning it has a lot of the depth of flavour and the body that comes from ageing, but without the sweetness and heaviness of a dark rum. It's very balanced. But there are loads of other great white rums on the market that might work better in certain drinks so don't be afraid to experiment.

Whether to use a white or a dark rum will be determined by the type of drink you're making but also by your palate. Richer, heavier, more alcoholic short drinks generally require the sweetness and depth of a dark rum, whereas a heavily citrussed or long drink needs the lightness and freshness that comes from a white rum, with its more natural acidity, but you might like a different flavour to me...

TEQUILA + MEZCAL

I don't have a wide range of either of these as they're not really something people ask for very often and I'd rather focus my attention on what people want. However, I do really enjoy drinking tequila. We stock one of each style – blanco, joven, reposado, añejo, extra añejo – and then we have a couple of mezcals. Although they're both made by fermenting and distilling the agave plant, mezcal is tequila's big brother. The main difference between the two, aside from the fact that tequila can only be made from a specific variety of agave plant and that they're made in different regions in Mexico, is that the agave used in mezcal is cooked over a wood fire in pits dug into the ground. This caramelizes the sugar in the agave but also lends the cooked plant a smoky aroma, which carries over into the mezcal, making it very reminiscent of a smoked Islay whisky. In fact I use them in the same way so if you're after a smoky flavour, you could definitely try swapping an Islay whisky for a mezcal from time to time.

I really like using tequila in cocktails because it has such an interesting flavour profile – it's grassy, herbaceous and has a high minerality (see pages 182–5 for more on these), which means that it's good at balancing out other elements in drinks. If you're curious and want to start to understand flavour more, then it's something I'd recommend trying. To make the recipes in this book, you're only going to need a blanco tequila and you're not going to be using it in big amounts, so it's going to last. I've bought Tapatio for as long as I can remember – there are a lot of excellent tequilas on the market, but I think Tapatio's has a fantastic flavour, particularly for the price you pay. For mezcal I like QuiQuiRiQui, but I mix mine up often as it's so diverse.

ABSINTHE

Absinthe carries this air of ambiguity and mystery, a bad reputation even, largely I imagine through misunderstanding and rumour. It was banned in the USA in 1912 because it was believed to be hallucinogenic, then a few years ago, it became legal again.

Absinthe is essentially a high-alcohol, anise-flavoured spirit. Its name comes from the scientific name for its key ingredient, wormwood. It's made in much the same way as gin: a neutral spirit is infused with a blend of botanicals, including wormwood, then redistilled. Traditionally, the alcohol is infused a second time to intensify the flavour and create its signature green colour, but a lot of modern producers skip this step and colour it with dyes.

I use absinthe a lot – we have it in a dropper and add tiny amounts to so many different drinks, but don't list it because it's used in such a small quantity. It has a fantastic floral, bittersweet quality. I add it to gin and tonics as it brings out the green flavours – essentially the herbs – in the gin; it lifts them. We make our own absinthe – a standard wormwood-based version, and a basil absinthe, but I've also made one with wasabi, for example. Just a 15-minute infusion of the herb or other flavouring can give it a really fresh, clean flavour. Have fun buying some samples and try experimenting with the different types.

COGNAC & BRANDY

Cognac is great in cocktails because it's a dark spirit but it has a fruitiness that you can bring out by pairing it with certain flavours; it's also used in some classic cocktails such as a Sazerac. I don't use it that often because there isn't a huge demand for it, but I keep one of each of the three categories: VS, VSOP and XO. I buy all our cognac from a small family-owned house called Réviseur and we also stock an English apple brandy and a Calvados, as well as some eau de vies. Again, just go for something you like or try a few samples and then choose your favourite.

FORTIFIED WINES, LIQUEURS + BITTERS

FORTIFIED WINES

Fortified wines are wines to which a distilled spirit, such as brandy, has been added. They range from dry, such as sherry and vermouth, to quite a large family of sweet wines, which includes port, Madeira and Marsala. Vermouth is an aromatized wine, flavoured with herbs, peels and spices, including wormwood. We've tried to make our own vermouth but it is a difficult product to recreate well and I don't see the point of making something if you can't make it better. There are so many amazing vermouths on the market that I'd prefer to stick to experimenting with and using those. I love a very, very dry vermouth and Regal Rogue's offering is my go-to for martinis. Something like Noilly Prat has an overtly wine flavour and more sweetness. Essentially, when you're picking a vermouth, the more expensive a product you're choosing, the more expensive a wine they've started with.

We also buy in other aromatized wines – these are like a vermouth but are flavoured with aromatics such as gentian and cinchona bark; they're set apart from vermouth because they don't contain wormwood, which vermouth historically has. Essentially, they're bitter wines that have been flavoured with sugar. They make great aperitifs on their own.

Aside from Regal Rogue, my brands of choice for vermouth and aromatized wines are Cocchi and Chinati Vergano. Cocchi's are simply crafted in a really good way; they use really good base wines and have won lots of awards in blind tastings. Chinati Vergano is much harder to source, but if you're interested in seeking out interesting flavours, they're worth investing in.

    The thing to note with vermouths and aromatized wines is that you've got to use them like wine, as they go off.

Sherry has had a renaissance in recent years. It's gone from being the drink your grandma had before dinner to one a lot of bartenders use. I use dry sherry a lot in cocktails – most often Tio Pepe's fino, for its dryness and because it's versatile, but I also like to use the darker amontillado and oloroso sherries because they've got different characteristics. Oloroso wines are exposed to more oxygen and they are richer and nuttier than finos. Generally they work well with dark spirits

ALL NATURAL
INGREDIENTS

100ML 30 %

HAND CRAFTED IN ENGLAND

BITTERS
ORIGINATED AS
A HEALTH TONIC IN
THE 1800S BY SOAKING
A VARIETY OF MEDICINAL
INGREDIENTS IN ALCOHOL TO
EXTRACT THEIR BENEFICIAL
ESSENCES. BOB'S BITTERS HAVE
BEEN CRAFTED WITH CARE IN
THE TRADITIONAL METHOD
TO ENHANCE COCKTAILS
USING THE FINEST
INGREDIENTS

WWW.BOBSBITTERS.COM

BOBS
BITTERS

NGE & MANDARIN

ALL NATURAL
POKE SMALL BATCH

BOBS
BITTERS

LAVENDER

ALL NATURAL
BESPOKE SMALL BATCH

BOBS
BITTE

CORIAN

ALL NATU
BESPOKE SMAL

and have a saltiness but without the biting dryness of a fino; you can add just a small amount and they change the back notes in a cocktail. We also use the sweet sherry Pedro Jimenez (PX) a lot in stirred drinks instead of sugar as it adds lovely raisiny notes.

LIQUEURS

We make our own liqueurs because I find most of the commercial varieties too sweet, so we make most of ours without any sugar. We just blend all the fruit with pectinase, which is the enzyme that breaks down the pectin in fruit and therefore helps extract their juices and creates a better yield. Then we centrifuge them to get a clean juice and add equal parts juice to vodka, to bring the ABV down, but also to make them really dry.

BITTERS

Bitters are made by macerating herbs and spices and infusing them in alcohol, generally a high ABV spirit. Once they've been macerated for long enough, the solids are strained. Bitters help accentuate flavour but they also bring their own flavour. The classic is Angostura (made from 90-odd herbs and spices but the recipe is a closely guarded secret) – it tastes very herbaceous and bitter; Peychaud's bitters is quite minty in flavour – it is bitter but less so than Angostura; and it now has colouring in it to make it red. Bitters are added very sparingly to cocktails – I don't generally add them to make things bitter; just to enhance flavour. Bitter cocktails come from their base spirit, such as Campari or a vermouth, not from adding bitters.

We buy Bob's bitters (Richard Peetree is a pastry chef; he started by flavouring sake and then moved on to bitters) and we have a huge range: cardamom, liquorice, grapefruit, chocolate, lavender, vanilla and four different types of orange bitters – we have a lot. In terms of what to stock at home – as a minimum you'll need an Angostura and a Peychaud, and then it's really up to you. Bitters aren't expensive so just experiment with them and see what you like. Bob's Orange and Mandarin bitters is a good place to start; it's particularly tasty, and makes an interesting change from a standard orange bitters, for example.

THE IMPORTANCE OF ICE

Making the right ice and having the right equipment to store it is pretty much the most important part of making a cocktail, and essentially it's a question of whether you have dry ice or wet ice. In a bar, if the ice that sits in your well (the insulated storage box that's built into most bars) is insulated and there's a lot of metal around it, it will stay dry when you put it into your glass or tin so you won't have to pour any water out. But if your storage vessel or your ice is too warm, for example, it will start to shrink, turn to water and then of course dilute the drinks.

In an ideal world, ice would be cut straight from the freezer as this method produces the clearest, cleanest cut cubes. However, at home, the best thing is simply to use ice cubes (from the freezer) with no holes. Ready-made ice cubes from a shop generally aren't good as they're rounded tubes with a hole in the middle, which increases the surface area and makes them melt faster.

For the best texture use ice cube trays that have the biggest cubes you can find, the bigger the better, although obviously not so big that it can't fit in your tin.

I go for silicone trays as it's easier to get the ice out. Fill them with filtered water, to minimize the cloudiness factor, and don't stack your trays – the trays in the middle produce cloudy ice as they freeze equally from all sides and trap dirt.

When it comes to making the drink, the key is the dilution; when you put ice in a tin, the tin is already warm – either from your hand or from the environment – so once you put ice in it the ice starts to melt straight away. We find it quite difficult to chill our tins as we're using them all the time, but at home you can put your mixing glass in the freezer for a short time before making your drinks.

With long drinks, ice is crucial. You've got to fit as much ice in your glass as possible, without getting what's called 'floaty ice'. When you put the ice in your glass, then pour your liquid in, you get to a point where the liquid starts to push the ice out of the glass. At that point you need to stop pouring and add more ice – that pushes the ice down into the bottom of the glass; it keeps your drink colder because there's as much ice as there can possibly be. You also need to make sure your cocktail is as cold as you can get it before you pour it in. In short drinks I tend to use just a single large ice cube as it melts more slowly.

INSPIRED BY INGREDIENTS

SOURCING

FORAGED + NATURAL INGREDIENTS

The ingredients I use and the way I think about them and treat them is at the heart of what I do. And it's the same way good chefs think about their food. Above all, my approach is driven by a desire to use ingredients when they're at their best, which means seasonally, with minimal travel. In the main I aim to use ingredients that are grown locally, working very closely with a forager.

Working with a forager provides me with a whole new range of flavours and ingredients to play with. Not only is it more sustainable, it's also stimulating, pushing all of us at the bars to be more creative. A bellini on the menu at one of the restaurants I consult for changes with whatever produce we get from our forager for instance. There's loads of beautiful fruit in this country that some people haven't even heard of, so foraged produce enables me to use flavours that guests haven't tried before, and I get to make a cocktail that's unique.

The way to think about ingredients is to work out how you want to use them and what for, then buy them. If you want a really clean, fresh flavour, then you buy and use something at the height of its season when it has just been picked. But if you want sweetness and a richer flavour, then wait for a fruit to be almost on its way out, when it has a maximum of sugar and natural sweetness.

The same goes for dried ingredients such as spices – they're at their most potent and aromatic when they're fresh, so use them promptly.

GARNISHES

Garnishes can be an important part of a drink but they need to make sense and add to it, either visually, with a flavour, or by complementing it with an aroma. Some of the garnishes I conceive are borne out of fun – I use cucamelons, for example (see photo opposite), because lots of people have never seen them, so finding a miniature watermelon perched on their watermelon drink is a novel element of surprise. But mostly I try to use garnishes that have a purpose; I don't like using a garnish just for the sake of it. One of the garnishes that got people talking and trying a drink was when I shrunk a packet of Monster Munch and pegged it to the side of the glass. We'd created a Pickled Onion Monster Munch Gibson by distilling the snack with vermouth and then making a classic Gibson, but of course the drink is clear. Pegging the little packet to the glass gave an understanding of the drink – a link between a colourless liquid and its flavour. It was fun, but also useful.

If you're putting a food-based garnish with a cocktail – it's generally there to be eaten. Sometimes it's even there to enhance the flavour of the drink. For example, I think a gin and tonic is greatly enhanced by garnishing it with a sea vegetable, such as sea fennel. We once made a drink inspired by a Portuguese soup, which was garnished with a wheat cracker that you were meant to bite and eat as you sipped the drink. The cracker was there to evoke part of the flavour from the original soup recipe, and without it the drink wouldn't have been 'complete'. A garnish can also be a way of adding a bit of texture – in the picture opposite (top right) I've gone for lychee-flavoured boba, the tapioca pearls used in bubble tea, which burst in your mouth and add something to bite into, as well as the juice from the inside and its flavour.

I generally like to put garnishes in the drink on a stick, but some things, such as herbs or edible flowers can be floated on top, and in long cocktails the garnish is often submerged in the liquid, which adds texture and in the case of something like pomegranate seeds, also provides little bursts of flavour throughout the drink so that each mouthful might be slightly different to the last. Herbs are another garnish that work well used in this way, an idea taken from the classic mojito, in which fragments of mint float throughout the length of the glass. Listed overleaf are some of the garnishes I turn to most often.

ORANGE AND GRAPEFRUIT TWISTS

Twists are a classic garnish for a good reason. They leave the top of a drink really fresh with an aroma that reaches you before you've taken a sip. You can either just squeeze the rind over the surface to extract the oil from the rind and get a lovely aroma, or add the whole piece of zest to the drink. I generally think just a squeeze is enough, particularly with martinis, otherwise you can overpower the drink with too much citrus and sour.

HERBS

I generally use herbs for their aroma, which adds to the whole sensory experience of drinking a cocktail. I often use sprigs of parsley, coriander (cilantro), lemon verbena and fennel fronds, and recently I've started using sorrel. The parsley and coriander (cilantro) are generally attached to the side of the glass using a small peg, mainly for their aroma, while the fresh sorrel is draped over the side of the drink so that you eat it and get a wonderful green flavour and a burst of acidity as you drink. When it's in season I use fresh sorrel in my Cherry Bark cocktail (see page 132), but I've also started making a sorrel nori, which we are able to keep for longer and use throughout the year when the fresh herb isn't available. Again, the nori adds a lovely acidity and a saltiness that contrasts with the barky nature of the drink. I use lemon verbena a lot, again for its aroma but it's also delicious to eat. It adds a real burst of herby citrus to a gin and tonic, for example. Fennel pollen and fronds I use particularly with drinks containing absinthe as the aniseed flavour in the herb brings the absinthe alive.

EDIBLE FLOWERS

I mainly use edible flowers for visual effect – apple blossom, borage, primrose and nasturtiums all add to and make the drink look pretty, but they can of course be eaten too. You just have to be careful with some flowers as they'll change the colour of the drink. Violas are often put into, or on top of, egg white-based drinks to colour the egg white purple, but that's not always the effect you're looking for. With short drinks I float flowers on the surface, but in long drinks they're often submerged.

SEA VEGETABLES

I love using sea vegetables, particularly sea rosemary and sea fennel. Sea rosemary is incredible – it's like a salty rosemary and I'll happily eat it alone. Sea aster and sea purslane are also great garnishes as they add a lovely hint of salt. I also use samphire. At Scout we serve a samphire water to our guests as

they sit down. It's just water that's been blended with samphire and mixed with a little malic acid but the flavour is amazing; it tastes like green apple.

VEGETABLES

Vegetables are a fantastic garnish both visually and because they're something you can eat. Radishes are beautiful but they also work well flavour-wise alongside strawberries in drinks, while cucumber, celery, pea shoots and slices of chilli peppers are all garnishes that feature regularly on my cocktails.

Essentially garnishes are about enhancing what's inside the drink rather than fighting against it.

EQUIPMENT+
TECHNIQUES

BASIC EQUIPMENT

A COCKTAIL KIT

The equipment you buy and invest in really depends on how much you want to get experimental and serious with your drinks and how far you want to go with them. So for that reason, I've divided this section into two categories: for the novice, i.e. the minimum of kit I think you need at home to mix drinks well; then equipment for the enthusiast. The latter are things we have at the bar that will take your drinks to the next level. Of course, there are things that could be added to this list depending on personal preference; many bartenders might consider a mandolin indispensable for example, but I'm not really a fan – I've sliced up my fingers too many times to feel they're really worth investing in. Either way, this list should be enough to get you started and help you decide what you want to fork out for, and what isn't worth it for you.

Dehydrated quince.

EQUIPMENT FOR THE NOVICE

MEASURING DRINKS

MEASURING JIGGERS (5)

Jiggers are the double-coned utensils you'll have seen every bartender use and they are essential for measuring drinks with precision. I use two different sizes and I recommend you do the same: a '25/50' gives you a standard single and a double shot (I buy the ones that have also got a 35ml (1¼fl oz) and a 15ml (3tsp) line inside); I also have a '40/20' which has a 10ml (2tsp) and a 30ml (1fl oz) line inside. Having both means you've covered all your bases in terms of the measures you'll need for making drinks. Try and go for jiggers that are tall and thin rather than short and squat as there is greater accuracy with the measures.

MEASURING JUG, SCALES AND SPOONS

You'll need a reliable set of scales, a practical set of measuring spoons (8) – mine are metal – and a measuring jug that's accurate, ideally one that can measure up to about 2 litres (4 pints), for making batches of liquid, but above all one that has small increments, which are more precise.

PIPETTE (11)

I often get asked about micropipettes, which are the pipettes used for measuring tiny amounts of liquid very accurately, but the truth is I don't use them – a normal pipette gives you consistent drops and that's enough for me. I'd only recommend a micropipette for extremely delicate flavours and that's not something you're going to find in these recipes.

MIXING DRINKS
MIXING GLASS/TIN (7)

Many bartenders use a glass for mixing their drinks, which works well and is relatively cost effective – you can buy very beautiful Japanese mixing beakers online. I use metal birdy mixing tins made by bartender Eric Lorincz. Metal chills drinks much faster and more consistently than glass, and even though you can't see the liquid inside, with time you get to know how much you need to stir to get the dilution required. Essentially, I think if you are consistent and use the same equipment to make the drink you will learn how to get the desired result.

BAR SPOON (9)

A bar spoon is the long spoon you'll need for mixing drinks because it reaches the bottom of your tin. The choice is up to you – just find one that feels comfortable in your fingers.

SHAKER

Although shakers can be divided further, the two main set-ups are the two-piece and the three-piece. The most common two-piece, consisting of two cups, one of which fits inside the other to form a seal, is called a Boston shaker (3). (You can buy tin on glass, or tin on tin, and as above, I'd recommend going for all metal.) A Boston shaker needs a separate strainer (10), while a three-piece, or Cobbler shaker (2) has one in-built. They separate into three pieces: a tin, a lid with the strainer and a cap to cover up the holes while you shake.

The choice of which to use is all down to technique and above all personal preference. I use a style of two-piece shaker, called a

Parisian (1), because I like the feel of them and they suit my style of shaking, but some of the guys I work with don't like them at all. If you go for a Boston shaker make sure you buy a sturdy one – you get a lot of cheap imitation ones that are made with very flimsy metal that sucks the parts together and you can't get them open. The Japanese Koriko shakers are a reliable brand – they are heavy and it's easy to break their seal.

STRAINERS

You'll need two strainers: a cocktail (10) or Hawthorn strainer and a fine-mesh strainer (6). The cocktail strainer has a spring around its edge that helps it fit snugly into different tins and mixing glasses, and a Hawthorn has two prongs at its top end, but it works in exactly the same way. However, the holes in these strainers aren't always large enough to strain everything you might need to, so you'll also need a fine-mesh strainer, which will allow you to 'double strain' and ensure you filter the smallest particles.

EXTRAS

CITRUS PRESS (SEE PAGE 73)

A good, sturdy lever-pull citrus press for juicing lemons, limes, oranges and grapefruit is indispensable – you can get green, yellow and orange ones for the different sized fruits. Given that so many cocktails require citrus, it's a good idea to buy the range.

SUPERBAG/FILTERS

If you're going to be making juices and syrups, you're going to need to strain them and for that I'd recommend buying a 'superbag'. They're most commonly used in professional situations by chefs and bartenders but they're really practical at home too. A superbag is a muslin bag used for filtering things – they're just more practical than using plain muslin cloths inside a strainer as they have handles so you can hang them up. Coffee filters are a good alternative when you need a really fine strainer.

COCKTAIL STICKS (4)

It might sound obvious but these often get forgotten – go for metal ones so that you can re-use them; I also prefer how they look.

SODA SIPHON OR A SODA MACHINE (SEE PAGE 73)

Both devices for making carbonated drinks, soda siphons are gadgets you attach to the top of a bottle to carbonate the water inside. They use a small CO_2 cartridge that you place inside the siphon. Soda machines are appliances that produce soda. They generally use a carbonator filled with CO_2 that is inside the machine and carbonates the water in a bottle that is attached to the appliance. I think they're easier and faster to use than siphons but they take up more space. Ultimately what you choose will come down to cost, space and how much you think you'll be making your own sodas rather than buying them. (For more on making soda, see page 200.)

GOOD ICE CUBE TRAYS

For a lot more information and advice about ice, see pages 52–3.

Overleaf: Page 72: Fine mesh strainer; Page 73 top left: Soda siphon; top right: Citrus press; bottom: Metal cocktail sticks.

GLASSWARE

HIGHBALL

A tall tumbler suitable for long drinks. As always, the choice is down to preference. I like a fine glass as I don't like heavy glassware, it feels cumbersome to me and I don't like it being thick in your mouth as you drink – the highballs I use, by Luigi Bormioli, are light to hold. I also like a short base – they have no window at the bottom of the glass so it looks like the drink starts at the table. In terms of size, I go for 250–300ml (8½–10fl oz) total volume.

ROCKS

A short tumbler, most easily described as the one you'd normally use to drink whisky. Again, I don't go in for the weighty, thick ones favoured by a lot of people – like the highball, mine have a thin glass and base.

FLUTE

For sparkling wines, I like small flutes with quite short stems – they're about 150ml (5fl oz) in volume. The glasses made by the Zalto glassware company are amazing – they have a really fine glass and an elegant shape and I like them because of how they feel in your hand. Sadly they are very expensive.

Although many consider that the flute's design makes it perfect for drinking champagne, I read a scientific paper recently saying that this isn't true at all – their smaller surface concentrates the bubbles which go straight up your nose and destroy the aroma of the drink. Wine glasses would apparently be better. But people's perception of what they expect to be drinking out of plays a huge part in their enjoyment of the drink. I can imagine getting some strange looks if I started serving champagne in a wine glass.

NICK AND NORA/MARTINI GLASS

Named after the protagonists in The Thin Man series of films from the 1930s and 1940s, the Nick and Nora glass (see page 96 for a photograph) is based on the ones used by the characters. The glasses Nick and Nora used were about a third the size of today's martini glass. We use them to serve all our 'straight-up' cocktails. I don't use martini glasses as I don't like them at all. Drinking out of them is really hard – the liquid spills – and so is carrying them on a tray. The Nick and Nora are becoming popular again so they're easy to get hold of and they look very elegant. The size of the Nick and Nora also means that provided your drink has been made well, it should stay cold for the length of time it takes to drink it.

SOUR/MANHATTAN GLASS

A sour glass is narrow at the stem and widens out towards the top. It's traditionally used for serving sours straight up, but I use it for lots of other cocktails served in the same way.

In terms of other glassware available or necessary, there are of course many different kinds, including wine glasses (useful for serving spritzs and spritzers), sherry glasses, coupes, liqueur glasses and sake glasses. The five listed here are the essential ones you should keep on hand for most purposes. We also have water glasses, which are halfway between a highball and a shot glass. As with so much, the glasses you buy will depend on what you like.

EQUIPMENT FOR THE ENTHUSIAST

BLENDER

Although this might seem like a basic piece of kit, I've listed it in this section because a blender that I perceive to be good enough is going to cost you between £600 (US$770) and £1000 (US$1285). I like to use a Thermomix – which heats the contents of the jug as you blend and allows you to warm things to a very specific temperature, under control and on a timer. I use it for making syrups – it's great for dissolving sugar as you can be really precise with it: you set the temperature, leave it for 7 minutes, say, and you've made a sugar syrup. We also use ours for grinding spices as it's really powerful. Some bartenders recommend a Vitamix as it is even more powerful but they impart heat and you can't control this so I wouldn't use one. An everyday heavy duty blender will do if you can't stretch to a more professional blender.

ROTARY EVAPORATOR

A piece of laboratory equipment used for distillation – it distills liquids in a vacuum rather than at atmospheric pressure, which allows you to distill them at a low temperature. I have one made by Buchi, which is Swiss and the oldest brand available. They also make ones that are fairly inexpensive (through they're still around £5000 (US$6440) for a brand-new one). You can also find them second-hand. Pharmaceutical companies sell them off, for example, and you can buy them on eBay for about £1500 (US$1930). For an enthusiast this is a great option for trying something at home.

Rotary evaporators are quite hard to use, but once you understand and know the basics they're really easy. The best thing to do is find someone who can take the time to show you. For more about distillation and why I recommend a rotary evaporator, see pages 82–3.

CENTRIFUGE

A centrifuge is a machine with a rapidly rotating container that uses centrifugal force to separate out ingredients according to their density. They spin the pulp from fruit to make juices, or the solids out of nut milks; we use also use ours a lot for clarifying syrups. The big problem for the home user is their size. The centrifuges we use at the bar are massive – with a 3-litre (6-pint) capacity they take up a lot of space and one of ours weighs about 150kg (330lb). You can buy a small benchtop one that sits on your kitchen counter that can do 300ml (10fl oz) and will give you an idea of what a centrifuge can do. They're fairly inexpensive – about £200 (US$255).

SOUS VIDE

To cook sous vide, food is placed in a sealable bag and cooked in a water bath. A sous vide is great for chefs and for us because it uses really precise temperature control to maintain flavour and nutrients, but they are also really useful in a domestic setting if you want to experiment with making your own syrups. We use ours for cooking harder fruits, such as rhubarb, apples

Opposite top left: Heavy duty blenders take away a lot of the labour of preparing fruit and vegetables.

Opposite top right: A centrifuge is often a large piece of kit, but smaller units are available for a domestic setting.

Opposite bottom: A rotary evaporator, worth investing in if you want to become a serious mixologist.

and pears – as it breaks them down and enables you to juice or centrifuge them more easily without damaging the flavour, but also mostly for cooking the foraged berries we buy – a lot are poisonous unless you cook them. Raw rowan tree berries are poisonous as they contain parasorbic acid, but if they are cooked well, the parasorbic acid turns to sorbic acid, which is not poisonous to consume. A water bath cooks the fruit without adding a lot of heat, enabling us to retain its freshness but still cook them at a high enough temperature to kill the poison.

VACUUM PACKING MACHINE

If you're buying a sous vide you'll need one of these – they're designed to seal foods in vacuum bags so that they're ready for the water bath. You don't need to buy a kitchen grade one, which would be very expensive – a small domestic one will do the job. I buy mine from the website www.sousvidetools.com – there is a good range for basic home use and the enthusiast.

DEHYDRATOR

Electronic dehydrators are machines that preserve fruit, vegetables and herbs by removing their moisture content. They're a pretty sizeable piece of kit, and the price tag reflects that, but I'm including them because if you want to start creating your own flavoured spirits and some garnishes, they're essential. Certain ingredients, particularly fruits, contain a lot of water, so if you're infusing a vodka, say, it will reduce the ABV quite considerably if you infuse it directly.

CENTRIFUGAL OR COLD-PRESSED JUICER

There are two kinds of juicer that produce a good yield: centrifugal and cold-press. Centrifugal juicers use a fast-spinning blade that extracts the juice from the flesh by centrifugal force, then directs the juice and pulp into separate containers. Cold-press juicers crush and then press fruit and vegetables slowly and therefore extract the biggest yield. The problem with centrifugal juicers is that the spinning generates a lot of heat, which destroys some of the enzymes in the fruits and vegetables you're juicing; and with cold-press juicers it's the cost. Cold-press juicers used to be really expensive – well over £1000 (US$1285) – but because there are more and more on the market now, the prices are coming down to around £300 (US$385).

FLOTATION HYDROMETER

We have an electronic hydrometer to measure the ABV of spirits, but at home all you need is a flotation hydrometer, which costs less than £10 (US$12) (versus electronic ones at £340/US$438). Flotation hydrometers are really easy to use, simply pour the liquid into a test tube, insert its float and wherever it comes to rest is where you measure the ABV. Their downside is that they're not hugely accurate, as your room needs to be at 20–21°C (68–70°F). Any hotter, and the reading won't be precise. We distill our own spirits, so it's vital we know the precise ABV, but unless you're distilling at home, and stopping before all the water has distilled, you're likely to be producing spirits at around 40%, so a flotation hydrometer will be accurate enough.

Opposite top left: A sous vide machine is used for preparing syrups.

Opposite top right: A cold-pressed juicer, used for large quantities of fruit or vegetables.

Opposite bottom left: A dehydrator is useful for preparing garnishes.

Opposite bottom right: A flotation hydrometer is a must-have piece of kit for measuring the ABV of liquid spirit.

DISTILLATION

Distillation involves heating a mixture of ingredients, typically water, alcohol and flavour – and converting them into vapour then cooling and condensing them back into liquid. There are two means of distilling: large-scale stills use atmospheric distillation, in which the liquids have to come to high temperatures to evaporate and became a vapour. We use a rotary evaporator for all our distillation which distills in a vacuum. The vacuum allows you to boil liquids at lower temperatures without any oxygen – it is the most gentle and controlled way of distilling something and prevents ingredients from oxidizing.

Laws in the USA make any form of distillation illegal – even in bars – and in the EU and Australia it is also illegal to distill alcohol at home for personal consumption without a licence, but it is legal in New Zealand. In the UK you are allowed to distill using a machine such as a rotary evaporator – and it's a vital process in my drinks. Distilling and creating my own flavours is at the heart of what I do and as such I have three rotary evaporators.

A rotary evaporator works on simple principles and once you get the hang of these the machines are easy to use. You pour an infused spirit – say a basil-infused vodka or a mixture of a spirit and another flavour, a juice or flavoured water – into the evaporation flask. Because something like basil is fresh, you don't want to cook it as it spoils and this ruins its flavour (it will taste over-stewed and musty), so you would distil it at a very low temperature – 50°C (122°F) – which you do by using the vacuum pump. It lowers the pressure inside the machine, which in turn lowers the temperature at which the liquid will boil. As you start the machine, you set your water bath to 50°C (122°F), the evaporation flask then rotates within the bath, and as the pressure comes down to work with the temperature of the water bath, the liquid boils at 50°C (122°F) and turns to steam. The steam then travels along a coil, which has a chilling unit that transforms it back into a liquid and this collects in a separate flask.

What you will have achieved is a beautiful, fresh, clear vodka that's flavoured with basil, and it won't spoil and go brown and oxidize as it would if you were simply infusing it.

Distilling allows you to create flavours that you want or need rather than relying on what's available commercially – we create anything from sweet potato vodka to peanut-flavoured white rum. We can't make whisky from scratch, of course, because of the ageing process, but when we buy a specific whisky and like its flavour profile and what it will achieve in a cocktail, we will often redistil it. This allows us to change it, add a twist to it and in turn create a totally different flavour profile for a classic drink. In our Super Soaker cocktail (see page 150), for example, we redistil American bourbon with watermelon juice, then re-combine it with some of the plain bourbon so that it still has the aged flavour of the bourbon but also a hint of watermelon. It means we can make a Manhattan cocktail from watermelon whisky – and the flavour is amazing.

We often distil rum with other tropical flavours typical of Tiki drinks, such as pineapple and coconut, and recently we've tried peanuts – we discovered that the fattiness of the nuts goes really well with white rum. We've distilled many things – even tequila – but most often we use distillation for flavouring vodka.

After you've distilled anything you'll most likely need to 'cut it' (add water) to reduce its ABV. To do this you have to measure the ABV of your distilled spirit then add water accordingly – in a very precise amount – to get to the ABV you want to end up with. I use a website to calculate the amount of water for me (www.homedistiller.org/calcs/dilute). It's really simple to use – you just input the quantity of spirit you have, and its ABV, and it will tell you how much water to add.

If you don't have distillation equipment, you can still infuse spirits, but you will add bitterness/salt/spice so you may need to play around with the recipe to get the right flavour. And make sure you use very clean water. Water can also add flavour, so use something with as little flavour as possible.

MODERN
COCKTAIL
RECIPES

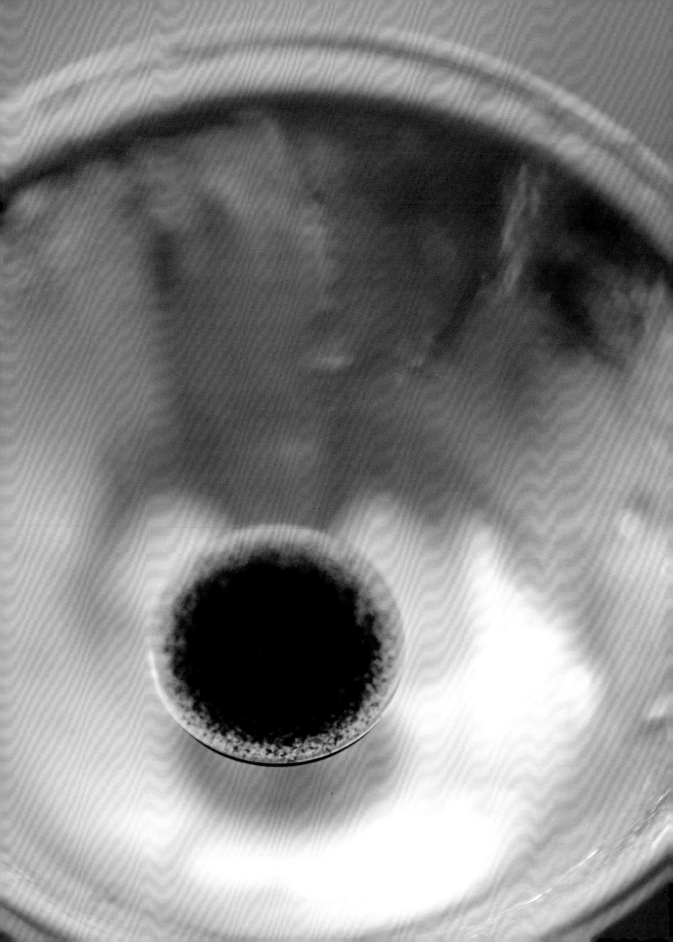

GIN

PEG LONDON DRY G&T *(Peg + Patriot)*

Cocktail type: long, herbaceous **Flavours:** bitter, sweet **Glass:** highball **Garnish:** sea rosemary or a slice of lime and a bay leaf	

This gin is something we stumbled across at Peg + Patriot. It was one of our seasonal gins and I liked the flavours so much that I decided to make it our standard London Dry.

I've suggested garnishing it with sea rosemary, which I know isn't the easiest thing to get hold of, but I'd really recommend trying it with this drink if you can. Sea rosemary is nothing like rosemary, it tastes like salt and pepper and I am completely obsessed with it. If you eat it alongside your drink, it really brings out the flavours. If you can't get your hands on it, adding a slice of lime and a herbaceous bay leaf would be a good alternative and another great complement to the drink.

Ingredients:

50ml (1¾fl oz) London Dry gin (see page 36)
135ml (4½fl oz) Fever–Tree tonic water

Pour a measure of the gin into the glass, add as much ice to the glass as possible and top with tonic water. Sit the garnish of your choice on top of the ice.

BURNT FOOL

Cocktail type: long, fruity
Flavours: sour
Glass: small highball
Garnish: dehydrated brown butter solids

This recipe was inspired by finding some rhubarb curd in the chef's fridge at One Leicester Street and wanting to recreate the flavours in a cocktail.

Ingredients:

50ml (1¾fl oz) brown butter gin (see below)
20ml (⅔fl oz) rhubarb curd (see below)
15ml (½fl oz) lemon juice
10ml (2tsp) egg white
Fever–Tree soda water

Pour the gin into a small highball glass and add the rhubarb curd, lemon juice, egg white and top up with soda water. Garnish with a pinch of dehydrated brown butter.

BROWN BUTTER GIN

Makes: 700ml (1½pts)

Ingredients: 50g (2oz) brown butter solids; 700ml (1½pts) gin

Place the ingredients into a vac bag and seal. Leave to infuse for 4 hours.

Place all the ingredients in the evaporation flask of a rotary evaporator. Set the water bath to 55°C (131°F). Slowly lower the pressure until all the liquid has evaporated. Measure the ABV and cut it to 40% (see page 83).

RHUBARB CURD

Makes: about 1L (2pts)

Ingredients: 600g (1½lb) rhubarb; 4 eggs; 200g (7oz) unsalted butter; 4 tbsp cornflour (cornstarch); 250g (9oz) caster (superfine) sugar

Juice the rhubarb. Add the eggs, butter, cornflour (cornstarch), sugar and 250ml (8½fl oz) of the rhubarb juice to a saucepan and set over a very low heat. Whisk until all the butter has melted, then stir constantly until the curd has thickened. Do not increase the heat to speed up the process, as the eggs will curdle. Pass the mixture through a chinois to strain, then bottle and refrigerate. This keeps for up to a month.

THE COLOUR BLUE

Cocktail type: long, minerally
Flavour: sour, effervescent
Glass: thin highball
Garnish: sea greens

Some people experience synaesthesia, a condition where a sensation in one of the senses, such as hearing, can trigger a sensation in another, such as taste. Just as some people can hear colours or taste numbers, I thought it would be cool to see what I could get the colour blue to taste like.

Ingredients:
40ml (1⅓fl oz) Bombay Sapphire gin
100ml (3½fl oz) fermented pineapple rinds (see below)
2.5ml (½tsp) seaweed distillate (see page 219)
50ml (1¾fl oz) egg shell soda (see page 213)
2.5ml (½tsp) 2:1 gomme syrup (see page 203)

Mix the ingredients in a glass bottle in the ratio of servings you need and pour from the fridge.

FERMENTED PINEAPPLE RINDS

Makes: about 5L (10pts)

Ingredients: 625g (1lb 6oz) brown sugar; 4L (8pts) filtered water; 16 cloves; 2 pineapples

Place the sugar and water in a fermentation bucket and stir to dissolve the sugar. Add the cloves.

Wash the skin of the pineapple and cut the pineapple into quarters, leaving the skin intact. Add to the bucket. Cover the bucket with muslin (cheesecloth) and leave it in a cool, dry place away from sunlight. After about 2–3 days the fruit will become cloudy and foamy. Scrape away the foam using sterilized utensils. Use the liquid when it has reached your desired sweetness. Save the pineapple triangles as a garnish or just eat them on their own – they're delicious.

MONSTER MUNCH GIBSON

Cocktail type: short, dry
Flavour: savoury
Glass: Nick and Nora
Garnish: empty, compressed packet of pickled onion flavour Monster Munch snacks

The classic Gibson cocktail is a martini made with gin and vermouth but garnished with a spring onion (scallion). This sarcastic take on it, created in collaboration with James Stevenson, involves making a vermouth flavoured with Monster Munch snacks and garnished with an empty packet that can either be shrunk in a hot oven (not fan-assisted) or lightly blow torched then pegged to the glass. The overall finish is strong and dry with distinctive pickled onion notes.

Ingredients:
50ml (1¾fl oz) Wolf's Nose hop gin
15ml (½fl oz) Monster Munch vermouth (see below)

Place both the ingredients in a mixing glass filled with ice and stir thoroughly. Strain and pour into a chilled Nick and Nora glass.

MONSTER MUNCH VERMOUTH

Makes: about 350ml (12fl oz)

Ingredients: 1 packet pickled onion Monster Munch; 350ml (12fl oz) Regal Rogue Daring dry vermouth; 100ml (3½fl oz) filtered water

Add all the ingredients to a large vac bag and seal it to the maximum pressure without spillage. Leave at room temperature for 4 hours to infuse. Once infused, strain the mixture and funnel it into a large evaporation flask of a rotary evaporator.

Set the water bath to 50°C (122°F). Slowly lower the pressure until all the liquid has evaporated. Measure the ABV and cut it to 40% (see page 83).

RÖK HOUSE BELLINI *(RÖK)*

Cocktail type: long, herbaceous, sparkling **Flavours:** savoury, sour **Glass:** flute **Garnish:** fresh dill pegged to glass	

This is like a salty, very fresh-tasting bellini. It's a drink I developed for the restaurant Rök, as one of their signature cocktails, which is also suitable for drinking with food. It sums up the restaurant quite well as they're very into fermenting and pickling, techniques which are mirrored in the drink.

Ingredients:

10ml (2tsp) fermented cucumber syrup (see page 206)
25ml (¾fl oz) dill-infused gin (see below)
90ml (3fl oz) sparkling wine

Stir all the ingredients together in a mixing glass then pour into a flute. Garnish with fresh dill.

DILL-INFUSED GIN

Makes: 300ml (10fl oz)

Ingredients: 300ml (10fl oz) London Dry gin; 200g (7oz) fresh dill

Add both the ingredients to a vac bag and seal to the maximum pressure allowed without spillage. Leave to infuse for 48 hours. Strain the mixture using a chinois and bottle.

STORY MARTINI
(Restaurant Story)

Cocktail type: short, fruity, herbaceous **Flavours:** sweet, sour **Glass:** Nick and Nora **Garnish:** tarragon and dehydrated strawberry	

The best way to describe this is as a salt and vinegar martini combined with the fruity flavours of strawberry and guava-flavoured vodka.
When creating it for Tom Sellers' Michelin-starred Story restaurant in London, I knew that Tom liked tarragon and I wanted to match that to a flavour that worked well with it; strawberry fitted the bill.

Ingredients:

25ml (¾fl oz) guava vodka (see opposite)

25ml (¾fl oz) Jensen's Bermondsey gin

15ml (½fl oz) strawberry vinegar (see opposite)

15ml (½fl oz) tarragon sugar (see opposite)

20ml (⅔fl oz) filtered water

1ml (¼tsp) saline

Multiply the ingredients up to the number of servings you need. Mix in a glass bottle then store in the fridge and pour straight from there.

STRAWBERRY VINEGAR

Makes: about 1L (2pts)

Ingredients: 750ml (1½pts) cider vinegar; 500g (1lb) fresh strawberries; 3g (1tsp) sea salt; 170g (6oz) caster (superfine) sugar; 2 lemons, juiced then skins added; 10g (2tsp) black peppercorns; 4 cinnamon sticks

Place all the ingredients in a vac bag and seal with maximum pressure allowed without spillage. Leave to infuse for 2 hours.

Place the liquid in the evaporation flask of a rotary evaporator. Set the water bath to 50°C (122°F). Slowly lower the pressure until all the liquid has evaporated. Measure the ABV and cut it to 40% (see page 83). Bottle.

TARRAGON SUGAR

Makes: about 750ml (1½pts)

Ingredients: 100g (3½oz) tarragon (leaves and stalks); 750ml (1½pts) filtered water; 300g (10½oz) caster (superfine) sugar; 6g (1tsp) malic acid

Place the tarragon, water and malic acid in a large vac bag and seal with maximum pressure allowed without spillage. Leave to infuse at room temperature for 24 hours.

Strain the infusion using a chinois and save the liquid. Add the saved liquid, along with the sugar, to a heavy-duty blender and blend at a medium–high speed. Strain.

GUAVA VODKA

Makes: about 1L (2pts)

Ingredients: 750ml (1½pts) Konik's Tail vodka; 500g (1lb) guava purée

Add both ingredients to a vac bag and seal with maximum pressure allowed without spillage. Leave to infuse for 2 hours.

Place the liquid in the evaporation flask of a rotary evaporator. Set the water bath to 50°C (122°F). Slowly lower the pressure until all the liquid has evaporated. Measure the ABV and cut it to 40% (see page 83). Bottle.

BASTARDIZED GIN MARTINI *(Rabbit in the Moon)*

Cocktail type: short
Flavour: minerally
Glass: tall Bick + Nora
Garnish: burnt lemon oil

The flavours of Asia in a martini. This drink came about when Michael from Rabbit in the Moon and I were having a chat about gin, and we decided to try and make an 'anti-gin'. In the conventional sense this isn't a gin at all, we simply put a tiny bit of juniper into the recipe to be able to call it gin, but it's mainly made with shiso, so really it's an Asian-inspired 'gin'.

Ingredients:

37.5ml (1¼fl oz) Beefeater gin
12.5ml (2½tsp) bastardized gin (see below)
5ml (1tsp) seaweed distillate (see page 219)
15ml (½fl oz) Regal Rogue Daring dry vermouth
30ml (1fl oz) filtered water

Multiply the ingredients up to the number of servings you need. Mix in a glass bottle then store in the fridge and pour straight from there. Garnish with burnt lemon oil (see below).

BASTARDIZED GIN

Makes: about 2L (4pts)

Ingredients: 19g (⅔oz) juniper; 30g (1oz) shisho leaf; 2g (½tsp) fresh kaffir lime leaf; 6g (1tsp) coriander seeds; 1 sancho pepper; 1L (2pts) ethanol

Blend the herbs and spices in a heavy-duty blender. Add the ethanol and leave to infuse for 4 hours. Strain then pour into the evaporation flask of a rotary evaporator. Set the water bath to 55°C (131°F) and distil all the liquid. Measure the ABV and cut it to 40% with filtered water (see page 83).

BURNT LEMON OIL

Makes: 500ml (1pt)

Ingredients: 6 lemons, 500ml (1pt) rapeseed oil

Heat your oven to 200°C/400°C/Gas Mark 6. Juice the lemons and collect the husks, then place the husks on a baking tray (sheet) and cook in the oven for about 1½ hours, or until black all the way through, checking them every 30 minutes. Leave to cool. Place in a Thermomix or heavy-duty blender along with the rapeseed oil. Blend for 10 minutes at high speed. Strain and bottle.

DUCK & WEAVE

VODKA

LESBURY DUCK — ANOTHER VODKA

70cl ▶▶▶ • ◀◀◀ 40% VOL

VODKA

MI-SO HAPPY

(Bone Daddies)

Cocktail type: long, fruity **Flavours:** umami, sour **Glass:** highball **Garnish:** pineapple leaf	

This is like a very loose, salty twist on a piña colada, using the savoury flavour of miso and other Japanese-inspired ingredients to sit alongside the theme of the menu at Bone Daddies.

For the clarified coconut milk I use the Koko brand as it splits really easily, producing a beautifully clear liquid.

Ingredients:

40ml (1⅓fl oz) Russian Standard original vodka

10ml (2tsp) sochu

50ml (1¾fl oz) clarified coconut milk (see below)

15ml (½fl oz) mango syrup (see page 205)

15ml (½fl oz) miso syrup (see page 205)

15ml (½fl oz) lime juice

10ml (2tsp) egg white

15ml (½fl oz) Fever-Tree soda water

Mix all the ingredients except the soda in a shaker over ice, shake and strain into a highball. Top up with soda and garnish.

CLARIFIED COCONUT MILK

Makes: about 750ml (1½pts)

Ingredients: 1L (2pts) coconut milk (from a carton); 60ml (2fl oz) lime juice

Warm the coconut milk to between 50 and 55°C (122 and 131°F.) Remove from the heat and add the lime juice. Stir. The coconut will start to split and separate. Strain the mix using a superbag. Bottle and refrigerate. Keeps for up to a week.

BANGKOK PENICILLIN

Cocktail type: short, spicy
Flavours: savoury, sour, aromatic
Glass: Nick and Nora
Garnish: prawn cracker

I've found that making sour drinks with Asian flavours works really well: Asian countries generally use a lot of acidity in their food so it's a logical mirroring. Making sours in this style is therefore sort of a signature of mine, largely because I love making the distillates – you can get a lot of flavour into them from the spices – but also because you can build a really balanced drink.

This one was designed to echo all the flavours in a Thai ginger chicken dish, which is something I love. It's also my twist on a Penicillin, which is a classic cocktail made with ginger and lemon juice.

Ingredients:
50ml (1¾fl oz) aromatic Thai distillate (see page 219)
20ml (⅔fl oz) ginger syrup (see page 206)
15ml (½fl oz) lemon juice

Shake all the ingredients with ice, then double strain into a chilled Nick and Nora glass.

PERFECT MARTINI

Cocktail type: short, dry, herbaceous
Glass: Nick and Nora
Garnish: orange and lemon twist

When you order a Manhattan, you can choose from a perfect, sweet or dry drink. A 'perfect' Manhattan has an even mixture of sweet and dry vermouth alongside the bourbon, and I wanted to think about how you could create a martini in the same way. The only way for me to do that was to distil the flavour of sweet vermouth into a spirit. The result is a wet martini but with the flavours of sweet vermouth.

Ingredients:
40ml (1⅓fl oz) sweet vermouth vodka (see below)
20ml (⅔fl oz) Regal Rogue Daring dry vermouth
1 drop Bob's orange and mandarin bitters

Stir together all the ingredients in a mixing glass, then strain into a chilled Nick and Nora glass.

SWEET VERMOUTH VODKA

Makes: about 1L (2pts)

Ingredients: 350ml (12fl oz) Cocchi di Torino vermouth; 350ml (12fl oz) ethanol

Place the ingredients in a large evaporation flask of a rotary evaporator. Set the water bath to 60°C (140°F) and slowly lower the pressure until all the liquid has evaporated. Measure the ABV and add filtered water to cut to 40% (see page 83).

TMF BLOODY MARY

| Cocktail type: long, spicy
Flavours: sour/umami
Glass: Nick and Nora
Garnish: thinly sliced dehydrated bacon and a cherry tomato |
 |

I was asked to do a pop-up bar at what was then the St John hotel (it no longer exists but it was an outpost of Fergus Henderson's – the chef behind the amazing nose-to-tail restaurant St John) and the obvious thing to me was to try and create a cocktail using the principles of nose-to-tail eating. I wanted to make a cocktail with blood in it, so a Bloody Mary with real blood seemed like a good place to start.

The blood I use is pig's blood. I buy it frozen in Chinatown in London but most Asian supermarkets will stock it.

Ingredients:
50ml (1¾fl oz) clarified spiced tomato (see page 210)
50ml (1¾fl oz) black pudding vodka (see below)

Stir the ingredients quickly in a mixing glass to reduce the temperature rapidly and not add too much dilution, then pour into a chilled Nick and Nora glass.

BLACK PUDDING VODKA

Makes: about 1L (2pts)

Ingredients: 175g (6oz) black pudding; 100ml (3½fl oz) pig's blood; 1L (2pts) vodka

Place all the ingredients in a vac bag and seal. Set a water bath to 70°C (158°F) and leave the bag overnight to cook the black pudding and blood. Strain and chill.

Pour the liquid into the evaporation flask of a rotary evaporator. Set the water bath to 60°C (140°F) and distil the spirit by very slowly lowering the pressure until all the liquid is distilled. Distil this one very, very slowly and carefully as the blood is quite volatile and can bubble up and overboil in the flask. Measure the ABV and cut to 40% with filtered water (see page 83).

APPLE
(Scout)

Cocktail type: long, floral
Flavours: sour
Glass: LSA highball
Garnish: apple marigold leaf

I was introduced to apple marigold by a farmer and just thought it was one of the most amazing herbs. I knew straight away that it was something I wanted to use at Scout. Its flavour is like a herbaceous green apple and I wanted to create a drink that played on its freshness. The result is this spritz-style cocktail. I buy our apple marigold from a grower called Westlands in Worcestershire.

Ingredients:

50ml (1¾fl oz) apple marigold vodka infusion (see below)

100ml (3½fl oz) lemon balm soda (see page 210)

25ml (¾fl oz) apple verjus (see below)

5ml (1tsp) 2:1 gomme syrup (see page 203)

Multiply the ingredients up to the number of servings you need and mix. Use a soda syphon to carbonate. I carbonate mine so that it's really fizzy. Store in the fridge and pour straight from there.

APPLE VERJUS

Makes: about 600ml (1¼pts)

Ingredients: 2 large cooking apples; 500ml (1pt) verjus

Peel the apples and cut into small 1cm (½in) pieces. Add to a vac bag along with the verjus and leave to infuse overnight. Strain and bottle.

APPLE MARIGOLD VODKA INFUSION

Makes: 750ml (1½pts)

Ingredients: 40g (1⅓oz) apple marigold; 700ml (1½pts) vodka

Add the ingredients to a vac bag and leave to infuse overnight. Keeps for up to two weeks in the fridge.

VIET SALAD

(Rabbit in the Moon)

Cocktail type: short, nutty
Flavours: savoury, sour
Glass: Nick and Nora
Garnish: lime zest, soy and sesame

Here I wanted to see if I could put all the classic ingredients and flavours of an Asian salad (apart from the fish sauce) into a sour drink.

Ingredients:

25ml (¾fl oz) Viet salad distillate (see page 123)

25ml (¾fl oz) Russian Standard original vodka

20ml (⅔fl oz) roasted cashew orgeat 5% 1:1 (see page 123)

10ml (2tsp) lime juice

30ml (1fl oz) filtered water

Place all the ingredients in a cocktail shaker. Shake and double strain into a chilled Nick and Nora glass.

VIET SALAD DISTILLATE

Makes: about 700ml (1½pts)

Ingredients: 400g (14oz) fennel; 50g (2oz) Thai basil; 10g (⅓oz) bird's-eye chilli; 700ml (1½pts) vodka

Blend the fennel, basil and chilli in a heavy-duty blender. Transfer to a vac bag, add the vodka and seal. Leave to infuse for 6 hours.

Set the water bath of a rotary evaporator to 50°C (122°F) and distil until all the liquid has evaporated. Measure the ABV and cut to 40% with filtered water (see page 83).

ROASTED CASHEW ORGEAT 5% 1:1

Makes: about 1.5L (3pts)

Ingredients: 50g (2oz) roasted salted cashews; 1L (2pts) water; caster (superfine) sugar

Blend the nuts in a heavy-duty blender for 20 seconds at a medium–high speed. Add the water and blend on a low–medium speed for 5 minutes, until all the nuts are fully incorporated. Strain through a chinois then fine strain.

Measure the liquid then add an equal part of sugar and return the mixture to a clean blender. Blend on a low–medium speed for 7 minutes, until the sugar has dissolved.

EARTH & TREES
(RÖK)

Cocktail type: short, dry, smoky, minerally
Flavours: savoury
Glass: Nick and Nora
Garnish: caper berries on a stick

This twist on a martini was designed for Rök smokehouse in London. It was based on a classic Scandinavian cheese and beetroot combination. The milky flavour comes from the birch sap and it's mixed with a burnt beetroot distillate.

Ingredients:

50ml (1¾fl oz) burnt beetroot vodka (see below)

5ml (1tsp) birch sap shrub (see below)

20ml (⅔fl oz) Regal Rogue Daring dry vermouth

Stir all the ingredients and strain into a chilled Nick and Nora glass.

BURNT BEETROOT VODKA

Makes: about 1L (2pts)

Ingredients: 1kg (2lb) beetroot, 500ml (1pt) 80% ethanol

On a barbecue, chargrill the outside of the beetroot until completely black. Set aside and leave to cool. Juice the beetroot and collect 500ml (1pt) of juice. Add the juice to the ethanol. Set the water bath of the rotary evaporator to 60°C (140°F) and distil until all the liquid has evaporated. Measure the ABV and cut the resulting liquid to 40% using filtered water (see page 83).

BIRCH SAP SHRUB

Makes: about 1L (2pts)

Ingredients: 350ml (12fl oz) birch sap; 350g (12oz) caster (superfine) sugar; 200ml (6¾fl oz) cider vinegar

Place the birch sap and sugar in a heavy-duty blender and blend for 15 minutes on a medium–low speed.

Once the sugar has dissolved, add the vinegar and blend for a further two minutes.

BOTTLE #1
TOMATO *(Rabbit in the Moon)*

Cocktail type: long, aromatic
Flavour: savoury
Glass: wine glass
Garnish: none

Although this cocktail has quite potent flavours – tomato and coconut – it has been designed so that they impart a subtle flavour and the drink should be enjoyed like wine.

Ingredients:

160ml (5½fl oz) Viet spiced vodka (see below)
130ml (4½fl oz) coconut syrup (see page 205)
100ml (3½fl oz) sour tomato syrup (see page 206)
25ml (¾fl oz) Russian Standard original vodka
195ml (6½fl oz) filtered water

Mix all the ingredients in a glass bottle and serve from the fridge.

VIET SPICED VODKA

Makes: about 350ml (12fl oz)

Ingredients: 1 cinnamon stick; 5cm (2in) fresh ginger; 3 tbsp fennel seeds; 1 tbsp coriander seeds; 2 cardamom pods; 65ml (2¼fl oz) oyster sauce; 3 cloves; 2 star anise; 500ml (1pt) ethanol

Blend all the ingredients except the ethanol in a heavy-duty blender. Add the ethanol and blend again. Transfer to a vac bag, seal, and leave to infuse overnight.

Place the liquid in the large evaporation flask of a rotary evaporator. Set the water bath to 60°C (140°F) and slowly lower the pressure until all the liquid has distilled. Measure the ABV and add filtered water to cut to 40% (see page 83).

CARROT
(Scout)

Cocktail type: short	
Flavours: sour	
Glass: Nick and Nora	
Garnish: slice of dehydrated carrot	

I love experimenting with combinations of flavour compounds to see what happens. Here I mixed the minerally peat flavours of hemp seed with sour carrot and liquorice to produce a delicate balance of earthy tones.

Ingredients:

35ml (1¼floz) hemp seed distillate (see page 219)

15ml (½fl oz) purple carrot vodka (see page 130)

25ml (¾fl oz) sour carrot juice (see page 130)

15ml (½fl oz) 2:1 gomme syrup (see page 203)

3.5ml (¾tsp) liquorice liqueur (see page 130)

10ml (2tsp) egg white

Shake and double strain all the ingredients into a chilled Nick and Nora glass. Garnish with the carrot.

PURPLE CARROT VODKA

Makes: 250ml (8½fl oz)

Ingredients: 50g (1¾oz) purple Chantenay carrots, finely sliced; 250ml (8½fl oz) vodka

Put the ingredients into a vac bag and seal. Place the bag in a sous vide machine set at 60°C (140°F) for 30 minutes.

LIQUORICE LIQUEUR

Makes: about 1L (2pts)

Ingredients: 100g (3½oz) liquorice stick; 1L (2pts) vodka; 200g (7oz) caster (superfine) sugar

Put the liquorice and vodka into a vac bag and seal. Place the bag in a sous vide machine set at 60°C (140°F) for 1 hour. Strain then add the sugar and stir until dissolved.

SOUR CARROT JUICE

Makes: about 500ml (1pt)

Ingredients: 1kg (2¼lb) purple carrots

Juice the carrots. Measure the quantity of juice collected and add a 2% ratio of malic acid. Stir to dissolve.

CHERRY BARK
(Scout)

Cocktail type: short, spicy, perfumed
Flavour: sweet
Glass: sweet wine or rocks
Garnish: sorrel leaf

This was created in collaboration with my Assistant Manager at Scout, Will Hetzel. Mastic is a resin gathered from the mastic tree and used to produce the brandy-like Greek liqueur, mastica. Whitebeams have bright red berries that are only available in late summer and early autumn, so like most of our drinks at Scout this one is very seasonal. Cherry bark gives it a light and delicate aroma.

Ingredients:

50ml (1¾fl oz) whitebeam distillate (see page 218)

10ml (2tsp) mastica

2.5ml (½tsp) cherry bark liqueur (see below)

5 drops lemon leaf tincture

1.25ml (¼tsp) 2:1 gomme syrup (see page 203)

7 drops citric acid solution (see page 203)

Stir all the ingredients over ice, strain into a chilled glass and garnish with a sorrel leaf.

CHERRY BARK LIQUEUR

Makes: about 1L (2pts)

Ingredients: 50g (1¾oz) cherry bark chips; 700ml (1½pts) vodka; 280g (10oz) caster (superfine) sugar

Put the cherry bark and vodka into a vac bag and seal. Place the bag in a sous vide machine set at 60°C (140°F) and cook for 1 hour. Strain then add the sugar and stir until dissolved.

BELLINI

(Rabbit in the Moon)

Cocktail type: long, toasted **Flavour:** savoury, sweet **Glass:** flute **Garnish:** caviar tin with lychee bob	

This new interpretation of a bellini is a combination of sparkling wine with green tea, a flavour combination that creates a savoury popcorn taste.

Ingredients:

10ml (2tsp) Genmaicha liqueur (see below)

115ml (4fl oz) Cocchi Brut vermouth

115ml (4fl oz) sparkling wine

Pour the Genmaicha liqueur and vermouth into a champagne flute then add the sparkling wine.

GENMAICHA LIQUEUR

Makes: about 500ml (1pt)

Ingredients: 50g (2oz) Genmaicha tea; 700ml (1½pts) vodka; 20g (⅔oz) per 100ml (3½fl oz) caster (superfine) sugar

Add the tea and vodka to a vac bag, seal and leave overnight, then strain.

Place the liquid in the large evaporation flask of a rotary evaporator. Set the water bath to 60°C (140°F) and slowly lower the pressure until all the liquid has distilled.

Add sugar in a ratio of 20g (⅔oz) per 100ml (3½fl oz) distillated and stir until dissolved. Measure the ABV and add filtered water to cut to 40% (see page 83).

RHUBARB

(Scout)

Cocktail type: fresh, piney **Flavour:** sour, sweet **Glass:** mirage or wine glass **Garnish:** none	

At Scout we make a selection of ferments that can be drunk just like you would drink wine, but they're something I'm playing around with a lot in other ways too. This is a simple play on the classic combination of rhubarb and custard. I've added pine, a flavour pairing I've picked up from chefs – it works really well with custard.

Ingredients:

75ml (2½fl oz) fermented rhubarb (see page 140)

35ml (1¼fl oz) custard distillate (see page 215)

7.5ml (1½tsp) pine liqueur (see page 140)

7.5ml (1½tsp) 2:1 gomme syrup (see page 203)

Stir all the ingredients over ice in a mixing tin and strain into a chilled mirage or wine glass.

FERMENTED RHUBARB

Makes: about 5L (10pts)

Ingredients: 3–4 kg (6¾–8¾lb) rhubarb; 800g (1¾lb) caster (superfine) sugar; 4L (8pts) water

Juice the rhubarb and measure out 1.5L (3pts). Stir the sugar into the water until dissolved, then pour into a fermentation bucket. Add the rhubarb juice, cover tightly with muslin (cheesecloth) and leave for 4–5 days.

Remove the muslin (cheesecloth), add the air lock and leave for a further 14 days, stirring once a day for the first 5 days. When the liquid has reached a flavour you're happy with, pour off the clarified liquid, being careful not to disturb the sediment. Bottle and refrigerate. Store upright.

After a while, any residual sediment will sit at the bottom. You can pour this off and discard or keep it in the bottle. Keep in the fridge for as long as you like.

PINE LIQUEUR

Makes: about 1L (2pts)

Ingredients: 15g (½oz) pine needles; 375ml (12fl oz) ethanol; 375ml (12fl oz) water; 280g (9¾oz) caster (superfine) sugar

Place the pine needles and ethanol together in a vac bag and cook sous vide for 30 minutes. Strain the ingredients through a chinois. Add the water and sugar and stir to dissolve.

PIKESVILLE

110 PROOF

REG. U.S. PAT. OFF.

STRAIGHT RYE
WHISKEY

110 PROOF (55% ALC./VOL.)

WHISKY + BOURBON

E2PA

Cocktail type: long, rich
Flavour: sweet
Glass: soda glass/small beer glass
Garnish: none

This was created at Peg + Patriot – hence the name E2, its postcode. We wanted to create a drink that looked like beer but was actually made from whisky. The burnt toast syrup, which is in fact made from chocolate malt but tastes like toast, is what gives it the dark colour and it makes it look like a stout.

Ingredients:

22.5ml (¾fl oz) Cocchi di Torino vermouth

7.5ml (1½tsp) Gonzalez Byass del Duque Amont sherry

2.5ml (½tsp) raspberry vinegar

20ml (⅔fl oz) hop distillate (see page 214)

10ml (2tsp) Woodford Reserve double-oaked bourbon

17.5ml (⅔fl oz) burnt toast syrup (see opposite)

0.008g charcoal

100ml (3½fl oz) soda

Shake everything except the soda over ice. Strain into your chosen glass and top up with soda.

BURNT TOAST SYRUP

Makes: 750ml (1½pts)

Ingredients: 75g (2¾oz) chocolate malt; 20g (¾oz) lactose sugar; 500ml (1pt) filtered water; 5g (1tsp) gum Arabic; 250g (9oz) caster (superfine) sugar

First blend the chocolate malt in a heavy-duty blender at a medium–high speed for 15 seconds. Add the lactose sugar and water and blend for 30 seconds at a medium–low speed. Strain the mixture through a chinois and collect the liquid. Clean the blender before adding the liquid back into it with the gum Arabic. Blend for 30 seconds at a medium–low speed. Add the sugar and blend on a low speed for 15 minutes. Strain and bottle.

WOODFORD REMAKE

Cocktail type: short, dry, fruity **Flavour:** sour **Glass:** highball **Garnish:** miniature apple	

When you go for training at Woodford Reserve, the guys there give you a taste of their unaged bourbon – it tastes like green apples. I wanted to recreate that flavour but using their aged bourbon. At the time I was working with someone who had asked me to distil kiwis, and it so happens that when kiwis are distilled they taste like green apple. So I distilled kiwi along with the aged Woodford Reserve to 'remake' the flavour it had before it was aged.

Ingredients:

50ml (1¾fl oz) kiwi fruit Woodford (see below)

12.5ml (2½tsp) 2:1 gomme syrup (see page 203)

10ml (2 tsp) Tio Pepe sherry

6 dashes malic acid solution (see page 203)

25ml (¾fl oz) Fever-Tree soda water

45ml (1½fl oz) Fever-Tree tonic water

Add ice to a highball glass, then build the ingredients in the glass and serve.

KIWI FRUIT WOODFORD

Makes: 1L (2pts)

Ingredients: 500g (1lb) peeled kiwi fruit; 1ml (¼tsp) pectinase; 1L (2pts) Woodford Reserve bourbon

Blend the kiwi fruit in a heavy-duty blender with the pectinase until smooth.

Measure the blended volume and combine with an equal measure of Woodford Reserve (about 500ml/1pt). Place in the evaporation flask of a rotary evaporator. Set the water bath to 50°C (122°F) and slowly lower the pressure until all the liquid has evaporated. Measure the liquid and add an equal part of Woodford Reserve.

METAL MAN

Cocktail type: short, dry, rich
Flavour: sweet
Glass: sour glass
Garnish: orange zest and cherry

This is a way of making a sweet Manhattan dry. You only need a tiny amount of the alum salt solution – alone it can dry your palate out in a single drop.

Ingredients:
50ml (1¾fl oz) L & G Woodford Reserve 43.2%
20ml (⅔fl oz) Cocchi di Torino vermouth
5ml (1tsp) Maraschino Luxardo 32%
5 drops alum solution

Stir over ice in a tin and pour into a chilled sour glass.

SUPER SOAKER

Cocktail type: Short, fresh **Flavours:** Sweet **Glass:** Nick and Nora **Garnish:** cucamelon, orange zest	

I worked on this with my bar manager at Peg + Patriot, James Stevenson. It's a take on a Manhattan – flavoured with watermelon to make it more thirst-quenching.

Ingredients:

45ml (1 ½fl oz) watermelon Woodford (see below)

30ml (1fl oz) Cocchi di Torino vermouth

1.6ml (⅓tsp) Campari

2 drops acid phosphate

Stir all the ingredients over ice in a tin, then strain into a chilled glass. Garnish with cucamelon and express the oil of the orange zest over the top, then discard.

WATERMELON WOODFORD

Makes: about 1L (2pts)

Ingredients: 1 small watermelon, peeled; pectinase; about 1L (2pts) Woodford Reserve bourbon

Blend the watermelon in a heavy-duty blender with 2ml (½tsp) pectinase per 1L (2pts). Measure the blended volume and combine it with an equal measure of Woodford Reserve.

Place the liquid in the evaporation flask of a rotary evaporator. Set the water bath to 50°C (122°F) and slowly lower the pressure until all the liquid has evaporated. Measure the liquid collected and add an equal part of Woodford Reserve.

PARSNIP

Cocktail type: short, rich
Flavour: sweet
Glass: rocks
Garnish: nettle leaf or popcorn shoot

A take on an old fashioned, this drink was developed in collaboration with Alan Sherwood, my bar manager at Scout. It plays on the buttery flavour of honey-roasted parsnips, hence the brown butter bourbon, but also uses parsnips' natural acidity, which makes it a fresh-tasting drink.

Ingredients:
15ml (½fl oz) parsnip bourbon (see below)
35ml (1¼fl oz) Bellamys #2 (brown butter bourbon)
6ml (1tsp) caramel syrup (see page 205)
6 drops Angostura bitters

Stir in a mixing tin. Strain into a rocks glass filled with ice and garnish.

PARSNIP BOURBON

Makes: about 1.5L (3pts)

Ingredients: 250g (9oz) unsalted butter; 1kg (2¼lb) parsnips, cored and quartered; 1.5L (3pts) bourbon

Melt the butter in a saucepan over a medium heat. Add the parsnips and cook until soft all the way through and deep brown in colour. Cool, then transfer to a vac bag, add the bourbon, seal and cook sous vide for 2 hours.

Place the liquid in the evaporation flask of a rotary evaporator. Set the water bath to 60°C (140°F) and slowly lower the pressure until all the liquid has evaporated. Measure the ABV and cut it to 40% with filtered water (see page 83).

WHISKY SOUR
(Rabbit in the Moon)

Cocktail type: short, aromatic **Flavour:** sour **Glass:** tumbler **Garnish:** ground espresso granules	

A simple twist on a whisky sour: the anise flavour of absinthe works well with whisky; coffee is another natural partner to whisky, and by making it into an oil I could give the drink some texture.

Ingredients:

50ml (1¾fl oz) Woodford Reserve bourbon

10ml (2tsp) 2:1 gomme syrup (see page 203)

10ml (2tsp) lemon juice

1ml (¼tsp) La Clandestine absinthe

5ml (1tsp) coffee oil (see below)

10ml (2tsp) egg white

Shake over ice and double strain into a tumbler. Garnish with the ground coffee.

COFFEE OIL

Makes: 250ml (8½fl oz)

Ingredients: 50g (2oz) ground espresso coffee; 250ml (8½fl oz) rapeseed oil

Place the ingredients in a vac bag, seal and leave to infuse for 3 days, then strain.

WINE + VERMOUTH

PEA WINE

Cocktail type: long, dry/herbaceous
Flavours: savoury
Glass: wine glass
Garnish: pea shoots

I developed this for the Fera restaurant at Claridge's, and it is still one of their most popular cocktails. I wanted to encapsulate the sense of a summer garden – fresh peas from a pod have a really evocative aroma – and here it is, distilled into a delicious drink.

Ingredients:
185ml (6¼fl oz) pea shoot distillate (see page 218)
185ml (6¼fl oz) Cocchi or Vergano Americano vermouth
375ml (12fl oz) dry white wine Riesling

Stir in a mixing tin over ice. Strain and pour into a wine glass. Alternatively, multiply the ingredients up to the number of servings you need. Mix in a glass bottle then store in the fridge and pour straight from there.

BLACKBERRY PINE

Cocktail type: long, dry
Glass: wine glass
Garnish: no garnish

My aim with Scout was to open a bar that created minimal waste and this is a drink that reflects that approach. Fermenting blackberries was a way of using up a load of leftover fruit we had at the end of the season and allowed us to make a drink that would keep.

Ingredients:

700g (1¾lb) caster (superfine) sugar
2kg (4½lb) fresh blackberries
6 long sprigs of pine

Pour 1L (2pts) of water into a ferment bucket, add the sugar and stir until dissolved. Add the rest of the ingredients, top up with water to make 5L (10pts) and stir again. Cover tightly with muslin (cheesecloth) and leave for 4–5 days.

Remove the muslin (cheesecloth), add the air lock and leave for a further 14 days, stirring once a day for the first 5 days. When the liquid has reached a flavour you're happy with, pour off the clarified liquid, being careful not to disturb the sediment. Bottle, refrigerate and store upright. After a while, any residual sediment will sit at the bottom. You can pour this off and discard, or keep it in the bottle. To serve, pour 125ml (4¼fl oz) into a wine glass.

SMOKED PEACH BELLINI

Cocktail type: long, smoky **Flavour:** savoury, sweet **Glass:** flute **Garnish:** none	

This flavour combination shouldn't work. Smokiness doesn't sit logically alongside sparkling wine, but smoking the peaches actually brings out a nice sweetness in them, and the brine from the olives balances that with a hint of saltiness.

Ingredients:

25ml (¾fl oz) smoked peach liqueur (see page 209)

100ml (3½fl oz) sparkling wine

2.5ml (½tsp) brine from black olives

Build the ingredients in the flute.

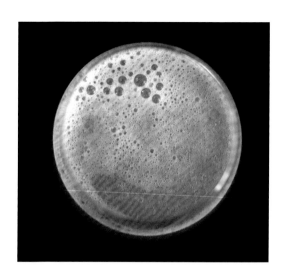

THOMAS WOLSEY

Cocktail type: long, fruity **Flavour:** sour **Glass:** flute **Garnish:** no garnish	

Cardinal Thomas Wolsey is the man credited with first putting the classic combination of strawberries and cream together, hence the name. I've gone for an Italian take on that concept, using ricotta instead of cream, and pairing it with Franchetto, an Italian sparkling wine, which has a lovely lemony flavour and brings a freshness to the drink.

Ingredients:

20ml (⅔fl oz) ricotta distillate (see page 215)

7.5ml (1½tsp) sour strawberry syrup (see page 204)

35ml (1¼fl oz) Franchetto soave

50ml (1¾fl oz) raw coconut water

3.75ml (¾tsp) 2:1 gomme syrup (see page 203)

3.75ml (¾tsp) Lemon verbena infusion (see page 210)

Multiply the ingredients to the number of servings you need. Stir them together, carbonate, pour into a bottle and serve from the fridge.

BIRDS	
Cocktail type: short, milk, aromatic, citrus **Flavour:** savoury, sweet-ish **Glass:** Nick and Nora **Garnish:** bay leaf	

Alexanders is a plant that grows on marshland on the outskirts of London. It tastes like a cross between fennel and celery, and this drink, created for Restaurant Story – is inspired by it. The Alexanders along with some of the other flavours are things that the birds on the marshland might eat.

Ingredients:

50ml (1¾fl oz) Alexanders, clementine and lemon sorrel (see page 172)

17.5ml (½fl oz) clementine liqueur (see page 209)

1ml (¼tsp) toasted oat (see page 172)

10ml (2tsp) Cocchi Americano vermouth

35ml (1¼fl oz) water

Multiply the ingredients to the number of servings you need. Stir them together, pour into a bottle and serve from the fridge.

ALEXANDERS, CLEMENTINE AND LEMON SORREL

Makes: about 1L (2pts)

Ingredients:
5 Alexanders bulbs (available from foragers)
3 clementines, rinds only
20g (⅔oz) wood sorrel
700ml (1½pts) vodka
100ml (3½fl oz) filtered water

Blend the Alexanders in a heavy-duty blender and transfer to a vac bag along with the other ingredients. Seal the bag to maximum without spillage and leave overnight.

Strain the liquid and add to a large evaporation flask of a rotary evaporator. Set the water bath to 50°C (122°F). Distil until all the liquid has evaporated.

Measure the ABV, cut to 40% with filtered water (see page 83) and refrigerate.

TOASTED OAT

Makes: 500ml (1pt)

Ingredients: 35g (1¼oz) oats; 500ml (1pt) vodka

Preheat the oven to 180°C/350°F/Gas Mark 4. Place the oats on a baking tray (sheet) and bake in the oven for 8 minutes or until golden brown. Remove from the oven and leave to cool.

Add the oats to a vac bag along with the vodka and seal it at the maximum possible without spillage. Infuse for 4 hours, strain and bottle.

FORAGED NEGRONI

Cocktail type: short, floral **Flavour:** bitter **Glass:** rocks **Garnish:** grapefruit twist	

Here I took the principles of a standard negroni but used foraged rowan berries to give it most of the bitterness that you'd normally get from the Campari, and added a floral note to it with St Germain to continue the 'hedgerow' theme. I tried using the St Germain liqueur but found it too sweet, so I distilled it to remove the sugar but keep the flavour of the elderflower.

Ingredients:

30ml (1fl oz) rectified St Germain (see below)

15ml (½fl oz) rowan berry liqueur (see page 208)

25ml (¾fl oz) Cocchi Americano Rosa vermouth

1ml (¼tsp) Campari

Stir all the ingredients over ice in a mixing tin then strain into a rocks glass filled with ice. Garnish with the twist.

RECTIFIED ST GERMAIN

Makes: 500ml (1pt)

Ingredients: 1 bottle St Germain elderflower liqueur

Place the liqueur in the evaporation flask of a rotary evaporator. Set the water bath to 55°C (131°F) and lower the pressure until all the liquid has evaporated. Pour off the distillate and bottle.

Save the sugar by-product and bottle to make elderflower syrup.

OTHER
DRINKS

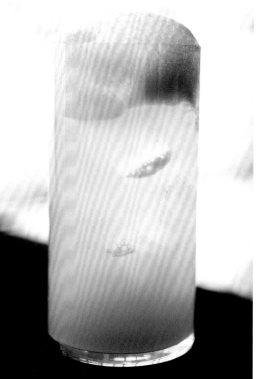

PEANUT COLADA
(RUM) *(Rabbit in the Moon)*

Cocktail type: long, rich **Flavour:** sour **Glass:** highball **Garnish:** none	

A twist on a piña colada, this drink is light and airy, with a mild-flavoured peanut milk used in place of coconut. The recipe for the banana syrup is adapted from Dave Arnold's.

Ingredients:
60ml (2fl oz) Plantation Pineapple rum
50ml (1¾fl oz) 3% peanut milk
35ml (1¼fl oz) banana butter syrup (see below)
10ml (2tsp) lime juice
10ml (2tsp) egg white
35ml (1¼fl oz) Fever-Tree soda water

Put all the ingredients except the soda into a shaker. Shake and double strain then pour into a highball filled with ice.

BANANA BUTTER SYRUP

Makes: about 750ml (1½pts)

Ingredients: 400ml (⅔pt) clarified banana juice (see page 192); 4g (1tsp) gum arabic; 2g (½tsp) xanthan gum; 500g (1lb 2oz) unsalted butter; 400g (14oz) caster (superfine) sugar

Blend the banana juice with the gum powders on a low speed in a blender until it turns to a gummy paste. Melt the butter in a saucepan over a low heat.

Add the butter to the banana paste and blend on full power until fully combined. Add the sugar and blend again until dissolved. Pass the liquid through a chinois, bottle and refrigerate. Keeps for up to a week.

SCALLOP PAIRING

(RUM) *(Restaurant Story)*

Cocktail type: short, fresh
Flavour: sour
Glass: milk bottle or wine glass
Garnish: dill

Designed to be paired with a scallop dish on Tom Sellers' menu at Story, this is packed with herbaceous hits and would make a refreshing drink prior to a meal

Ingredients:

16ml (½fl oz) cucumber rum
5ml (1tsp) burnt dill rum (see below)
15ml (½fl oz) 2:1 gomme syrup (see page 203)
10ml (2tsp) Tio Pepe sherry
28ml (1fl oz) malic acid solution (see page 203)

Multiply the ingredients up to the number of servings you need. Mix in a glass bottle then store in the fridge, leave until chilled and pour straight from there.

BURNT DILL RUM

Makes: about 700ml (1½pts)

Ingredients: 300g (10½oz) dill; 700ml (1½pts) white rum

Preheat your oven on its lowest setting. Spread the dill evenly over a baking tray (sheet) and bake in the oven for 3-6 hours or until completely dry (or dehydrate in a dehydrator on a medium heat for 6 hours). Place the dehydrated dill on a large, deep baking tray (sheet) and use a blow torch to burn the dill until it's completely black.

Place the burnt dill and rum in a vac bag and seal to the maximum allowed without leaking. Leave to infuse overnight.

Pour the liquid into the evaporation flask of a rotary evaporator. Set the water bath to 55°C (131°F) and lower the pressure until all the liquid has evaporated. Measure the ABV and cut to 40% with filtered water (see page 83) then bottle.

MARGARITA
(TEQUILA) *(Rabbit in the Moon)*

Cocktail type: short, fresh, minerally **Flavour:** sour **Glass:** sour glass **Garnish:** lime zest	

One of the things I like about distilling chilli is that you get all its fresh flavour without any heat. When you smell the distillate, it smells as if it's going to taste really spicy, and then you drink it and it has no heat whatsoever. It messes with your senses a little bit.

Ingredients:

50ml (1¾fl oz) Tapatio Blanco tequila

20ml (⅔fl oz) Cointreau

10ml (2tsp) lime juice

25ml (¾fl oz) green chilli tincture (see below)

Stir in a mixing tin over ice and pour into a chilled sour glass. Garnish with lime zest.

GREEN CHILLI TINCTURE

Makes: 1L (2pts)

Ingredients: 1.2kg (2½lb) fresh jalapeño peppers; 2ml (½tsp) pectinase; 375ml (12fl oz) Tapatio Blanco tequila

Blend the whole chillies with the pectinase until smooth. Place in a vac bag with the tequila and leave to infuse overnight.

Pour the liquid into the evaporation flask of a rotary evaporator. Set the water bath to 50°C (122°F) and lower the pressure until all the liquid has evaporated.

Please note that this is not something you can infuse, you have to distil the chilli and tequila; an infusion would blow your socks off!

LACK OF FAITH
(TEQUILA)

Cocktail type: short **Flavour:** savoury, dry, smoky **Glass:** liqueur glass **Garnish:** grapefruit zest (discarded)	

One of my bar staff was really keen to make a drink using roasted artichokes, but she had no faith in her ability to create a recipe. In the end our whole team got involved to make suggestions as to what would work, and it turned out to be a real success.

Ingredients:

20ml (⅔fl oz) burnt artichoke tequila (see below)

20ml (⅔fl oz) Cocchi Americano vermouth

20ml (⅔fl oz) Beefeater gin

2.5ml (½tsp) grapefruit liqueur (see page 209)

0.1ml saline solution

0.025ml Bob's vanilla bitters

Stir the ingredients in a mixing tin over ice and strain into a chilled liqueur glass. Express the zest of the grapefruit and discard.

BURNT ARTICHOKE TEQUILA

Makes: about 750ml (1½pts)

Ingredients: 1 globe artichoke; 700ml (1½pts) Tapatio Blanco tequila

Preheat the oven to 200°C/400°F/Gas Mark 6. Place the artichokes on a baking tray (sheet) and roast them whole for 30 minutes. Remove and leave to cool.

Cut off the artichoke stalk, then peel the leaves. Cut the heart in half and remove the hairy choke, then discard, along with the stalk. Blitz the leaves and heart in a heavy-duty blender, then slowly add the tequila in batches, continuing to blend. Transfer to a vac bag and leave to infuse for 4 days in the fridge.

Pour the liquid into the evaporation flask of a rotary evaporator. Set the water bath to 65°C (149°F) and lower the pressure until all the liquid has evaporated.

GRONER
SAZERAC (COGNAC)

Cocktail type: short, dry **Flavour:** savoury **Glass:** tumbler **Garnish:** a micropipette of mustard leaf infusion	

When we started out at Peg + Patriot, I wanted to make drinks that reflected or were reminiscent of the local area. Bethnal Green has a strong Jewish heritage, while my wife's family used to have a Jewish restaurant on nearby Brick Lane called D. Groner. I created this sazerac, made from a distillate of salt beef, as a nod to both.

Ingredients:

15ml (½fl oz) salt beef distillate (see page 214)

25ml (¾fl oz) cognac

5ml (1tsp) 2:1 gomme syrup (see page 203)

5 drops Peychaud's aromatic bitters

Stir in a mixing tin, then pour into a tumbler filled with ice and garnish.

PRETZEL MANGER
(COGNAC)

Cocktail type: short, nutty, dry
Flavour: savoury
Glass: sweet wine or rocks
Garnish: shiso leaf

For a Talented Mr Fox pop-up I wanted to make a sazerac-style drink that had fun, sweet elements like peanut butter and pretzels, but was in fact quite 'grown-up' and refined. This sounds like it is going to be really rich and sweet, when actually it's a nutty, dry drink.

Ingredients:

20ml (⅔fl oz) pretzel and peanut butter distillate (see page 219)

15ml (½fl oz) Domaine le Reviseur VS Petite cognac

15ml (½fl oz) Rittenhouse 100 proof rye

2ml (½ tsp) La Clandestine absinthe

10ml (2 tsp) clarified pear syrup (see page 204)

Stir the ingredients in a mixing tin over ice. Strain into a chilled glass and garnish with the shiso leaf.

TURKISH COFFEE
(RAKI)

Cocktail type: short, aromatic
Flavour: umami
Glass: coupe
Garnish: cardamom seeds

This is something I was asked to create for a Turkish restaurant. It is basically an espresso martini but uses the anise flavour of raki in place of vodka as it works so well with coffee.The caramelized yoghurt syrup adds texture.

Ingredients:
45ml (1½fl oz) coffee raki (see below)
25ml (¾fl oz) caramelized yoghurt (see below)
3 drops Bob's cardamom bitters

Shake really well over ice, then double strain into a chilled glass.

COFFEE RAKI

Makes: about 1L (2pts)

Ingredients: 1L (2pts) raki; 100g (3½oz) coarsely ground coffee granules

Put the raki and coffee into a large vac bag and seal. Leave for 1 hour then strain through coffee filter paper. Bottle.

CARAMELIZED YOGHURT

Makes: about 1L (2pts)

Ingredients: 500g (1lb) Greek yoghurt; 500g (1lb) caster (superfine) sugar

Place the ingredients in a blender and blitz until smooth, then transfer to a vac bag and seal. Set a sous vide to 85°C (185°F) (be careful). When the water bath has reached temperature, add the vac bag and set a timer for 20 hours. At this point the yoghurt should be brown and have the consistency of *dulce de leche*.Strain and bottle.

CLARIFIED BANANA JUICE

Makes: 750ml–1L (1½–2pts)

Ingredients: 2kg (4½lb) peeled bananas; 2ml (½ tsp) pectinase

Blend the banana and pectinase in batches in a high-speed blender for 5 minutes until liquid. Pour the liquid into a large jug.

In a centrifuge, divide the liquid evenly between the buckets and spin at 4000 rpm for 20 minutes. Pour off the clarified juice and strain through a muslin (cheesecloth).

Bottle and store in the fridge for up to 3 days (you can keep it longer, but it starts to brown).

BOTTLE #2
BANANA (SAKE)

Cocktail type: long, fresh
Flavour: savoury, sweet
Glass: flute
Garnish: none

When you make the clarified banana juice for this one, please note that the centrifuge will cause the banana collected to split into layers. There will be a hard disc at the bottom, then a liquid layer and then another solid disc. For the purposes of the pictures opposite, I put
my finger into the bottle to push the disc down and allow the liquid to run out, but I wouldn't advise doing this; and if you do, make sure your hands are really clean. Normally the type of centrifuge bucket I use would prevent this from being necessary.

Though it sounds like a weird combination, banana and parsley are closely linked in terms of their compounds. Savoury from the sake, sweet from the banana, with a hint of green from the parsley – honestly, this drink is delicious.

Ingredients:

75ml (2½fl oz) Honjozo-shu sake
50ml (1¾fl oz) clarified banana juice (see opposite)
10ml (2tsp) parsley distillate (see page 217)

Mix the total number of servings in a jug then store in the fridge until ready to serve.

BOTTLE #3 RICE
(SAKE) *(Rabbit in the Moon)*

Cocktail type: long, aromatic
Flavour: sour
Glass: flute
Garnish: none

I wanted to make a sake with the flavour of yuzu without actually buying the fruit as it's really expensive. Calamansi – a cross between a mandarin and a kumquat – has a very similar flavour profile but costs a lot less.

Ingredients:
150ml (5fl oz) sake
15ml (½fl oz) mangosteen syrup (see below)
2.5ml (½tsp) calamansi purée (defrosted if using frozen)

Mix all the ingredients together and pour into a chilled flute.

MANGOSTEEN SYRUP

Makes: 750ml (1½pts)

Ingredients: 1.5kg (3⅓lb) mangosteen; 500g (1lb) caster (superfine) sugar; 500ml (1pt) filtered water

Cut the mangosteens in half and remove the fruit from the inside. Blend all the ingredients in a heavy-duty blender until the sugar has dissolved. Strain.

SYRUPS, LIQUEURS, SODAS, JUICES, INFUSIONS + DISTILLATES

USING MY RECIPES

With most processes in drinks making, there's the way I do things, which is aimed at extracting optimum flavour and creating beautiful visual effects, such as clarity in my drinks, and then there are ways that are more achievable at home. I use a lot of fancy, often expensive equipment, but when you're starting out you don't need to buy all of this; there are ways of adapting many of the processes in the recipes. You can infuse spirits with flavour instead of distilling them (except in some instances where I've specified it's not possible as the flavour just cannot be replicated through infusion); and you can fine-strain liquids through a superbag (see page 71) instead of centrifuging them – it's simply that the end result won't be quite as clear as if you follow the advanced technique, and the processes will take quite a bit longer.

This book isn't about making things prohibitively difficult – what I really want you to take from it is a desire to experiment with flavour – to think beyond conventional perceptions of flavour boundaries and just to try things. I can't guarantee the results will be perfect or as I intended them all of the time, but hopefully you will have some fun learning and create some great drinks of your own too. That's how I started...

BASIC TECHNIQUES

SYRUPS

There are two different types of syrup: two-parts-sugar-to-one-part-water, or equal parts. Essentially a lot of what you choose will come down to your palate, but we use both methods. Our basic sugar syrup is two-to-one, which is of course extremely sugary, but we use it very sparingly – a little bit goes a long way – so rather than adding more volume to a drink and changing the ratio of the liquid, we use just a very small amount.

When we make flavoured syrups, such as fruit syrups, we use a one-to-one syrup because the flavour then becomes part of the drink and you might need to use more of it. At home, I'd recommend making all syrups using a one-to-one ratio so that you don't oversweeten things.

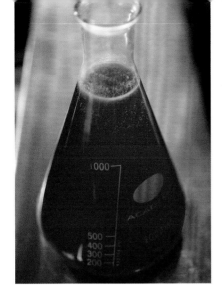

At the bar I will use a centrifuge to make most fruit or vegetable syrups, but that's simply because I have one and it means I can produce a very clear, clean syrup. At home you really don't need to do that. The simplest way to make a syrup is to measure the fruit's weight and add half that weight in water to it, then blend it. The water obviously dilutes the flavour but it also increases the yield. Leave it to strain through a chinois lined with muslin (cheesecloth) or a superbag but don't touch it – don't press it at all or you'll push through solids, so just let it sit and drain. We then add pectinase (I use a brand called Pectinex, see page 220 for where to source it), a fruit enzyme that breaks down pectin sugars and therefore increases yield and improves the clarity of the syrup, but you don't need to do this. There's no specific quantity to add; a little bit goes a long way so just start by adding a tiny amount – no more than 2ml (½tsp) – and just keep adding until you get your syrup as clear as you want. Then weigh the liquid again and mix it with the same weight of caster (superfine) sugar, then heat it very, very gently – just enough to warm it through and dissolve the sugar.

The other thing to note is that you don't always have to juice or blend your own fruit to make a syrup. There are some really good fresh juices available to buy and they open up a whole range of flavours. Good supermarkets and food stores have a great selection; Waitrose does a really good mango juice and an amazing blood orange juice, for example, and all you do is mix the juice with an equal part of sugar and heat as above. Just experiment – try a watermelon juice and see what you get, then try mixing it with a smoky whisky or a sparkling wine.

LIQUEURS

I find most of the commercial varieties of liqueur too sweet, so by making our own we can control the amount of sugar. As with syrups, we blend the fruit with

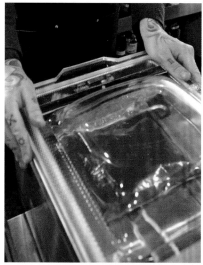

A vac pac machine is invaluable for making infused liquids in flavour combinations that you can't readily buy. We then carbonate them and turn them into sodas.

Place your ingredients in a vac bag, seal and leave for several hours or overnight for all the flavours to infuse together and create a base for sodas or liqueurs.

pectinase then we centrifuge the blended fruit to get a clarified juice (as with the syrups, you can skip this part at home) and add equal parts juice to vodka or ethanol, depending on the ABV I'm looking for. If I want the ABV to be around 40%, I'll use ethanol. The ethanol I use has an ABV of 79.8%, so once I've added it to an equal quantity of blended fruit, the ABV will come down to around 40% (though that's still high for a liqueur). With vodka, the final ABV will be around 20%. I'll also add water to bring the ABV down (known as cutting), as you'll see in some of these recipes.

Some liqueurs have nice residual sugar so I don't sweeten them. Raspberries have a natural sourness and a dryness, which I like to work with, so I don't add any sugar to them, but you may want to add a little. Some fruits will need some sugar – rowan berries, for example. In that case I'll generally add between 10–20g (¼–¾oz) of sugar per 100ml (3½fl oz) of liquid. When you're making your own liqueurs, start with a low quantity of sugar and then add about 2g (½tsp) of sugar per 100ml (3½fl oz) of liquid until you have a flavour you're happy with.

SODAS

At the bars we make our own sodas because it allows us to make flavours you can't buy, like parsley or plum soda. We carbonate directly from big canisters of CO_2 but you can easily make sodas at home using a soda siphon or machine by making a flavoured syrup then adding it to water and carbonating it, or flavouring the water directly then carbonating. Again, having a carbonating facility will allow you to play with flavours.

If you have a vac pac machine, for example, you can put a large handful of parsley in water, seal it in the machine and leave it for a few hours at room temperature. The water will take on a lot of parsley flavour, so you then strain it, add a little bit of caster (superfine) sugar, sweetening it to taste (or not), then carbonate it in a soda siphon. It's delicious and there are so many opportunities for trying different fruits, vegetables and other herbs.

INFUSING ALCOHOL

There's not really an all-encompassing recipe or technique for how to infuse an alcohol as it really depends on the ingredient you're infusing and the strength of its flavour. Infusing is really about understanding that flavour and then learning to work with it. Some herbs, say dill, will have quite a potent flavour when really fresh or just picked, but sometimes they will have very little. Where possible it's about tasting your ingredient and seeing how much taste you get in your mouth and then working out the infusing process from there. The best way is to try a couple of the more basic recipes in this book and then experiment once you get more confident. As a very rough guide, when infusing a herb I would use between 10 and 15 per cent of the weight of the spirit; with spices this would drop to 5 per cent.

Wash the ingredient thoroughly and leave it in the spirit overnight at room temperature. Taste the spirit to check the flavour then either strain the ingredient or leave it infusing for a bit longer to deepen the flavour.

SMOKING

Smoking might sound like something that needs to be done outdoors, but it's actually very contained and easy to do. We have a benchtop smoker that you use over a hob (stovetop). It has a small tray for holding your ingredient and a tray at the bottom for the woodchips. The woodchips are tiny and you don't need very many. Scatter them across the tray – fairly evenly so that the smoke isn't all in one place, then put your ingredient into the top tray. Put the smoker on the hob (stovetop) on a medium heat and wait for the woodchips to catch. As it starts to smoke, move the tray around so that the heat isn't all in one place. Smoke things for as long as you like. I like things quite smoky, so, for the smoked peaches in the Smoked Peach Bellini (see page 166) I'd smoke them for 10–15 minutes, but you can start with less depending on how smoky you like things.

BASIC RECIPES

All the recipes in this section will add balance to drinks. The spirit is the main part of a cocktail; these recipes add acidity (acid solutions), salt, sweetness and bitterness – a bit like the way chefs use salt and pepper for seasoning, they all change and adjust flavour. I know there are a lot of flavoured syrups, but I really believe that if you're adding a sugar syrup, why not add something flavoured to give the drink a different dimension. If you've got a drink that's too acidic and you're simply trying to reduce that, you don't want to add flavour, so you just need a plain sugar syrup.

As their names suggest, the acid solutions both simply add acidity; citric has a more floral flavour; malic acid comes from apples and is cleaner. I generally use malic acid.

MALIC ACID SOLUTION

Makes: 80ml (2¾fl oz) (you only need enough to use as drops)

Used in: Woodford Remake, Whisky + Bourbon (page 144); Scallop Pairing, Rum (page 180)

Ingredients:
20g (¾oz) powdered malic acid
80ml (2¾fl oz) filtered water

Stir the acid into the water until dissolved. You can store this at room temperature.

CITRIC ACID SOLUTION

Makes: 80ml (2¾fl oz) (you only need enough to use as drops)

Used in: Cherry Bark, Vodka (page 134)

Ingredients:
20g (¾oz) powdered citric acid
80ml (2¾fl oz) filtered water

Stir the acid into the water until completely dissolved. You can store this at room temperature.

2:1 GOMME SYRUP

Makes: 1L (2pts)

Used in: The Colour Blue, Gin (page 92); Apple, Vodka (page 118); Carrot, Vodka (page 128); Cherry Bark, Vodka (page 134); Rhubarb, Vodka (page 136); Woodford Remake, Whisky + Bourbon (page 144); Whisky Sour, Whisky + Bourbon (page 155); Thomas Wolsey, Wine + Vermouth (page 168); Scallop Pairing, Rum (page 181); Groner Sazerac, Cognac (page 186)

Ingredients:
1L (2pts) filtered water
2kg (4½lb) caster (superfine) sugar
1g (a pinch) gum Arabic

Mix ingredients together and bottle. Keeps for up to a month.

FRUIT + VEGETABLE SYRUPS

Most fruit syrups are a ratio of 1:1 fruit to sugar because they're naturally sweet and I don't want them to taste like candy. Some, such as the sour strawberry don't have any added sugar at all. All syrups can be stored for up to two weeks in the fridge.

SOUR STRAWBERRY SYRUP

Makes: 500ml (1pt)

Used in: Thomas Wolsey, Wine + Vermouth (page 168)

Ingredients:
1kg (2¼lb) strawberries
citric acid
malic acid

Juice the strawberries. Distribute the juice evenly between the centrifuge buckets of your machine and spin at 4000 rpm for 20 minutes.

Pour the mixture into a measuring jug. For every 94ml (3fl oz) of juice you will need to add 4g (1tsp) of citric acid and 2g (½tsp) of malic acid. Stir until dissolved. Keep in the fridge and use within two weeks.

CLARIFIED PEAR SYRUP

Makes: 1L (2pts)

Used in: Pretzel Manger, Cognac (page 188)

Ingredients:
1L (2pts) organic pear juice
caster (superfine) sugar

Distribute the juice evenly between the centrifuge buckets of your machine. Spin at 3500 rpm for 20 minutes. Pour off the clarified juice and measure.

Add equal parts juice to sugar in a heavy-duty blender and blend until completely smooth. Bottle and refrigerate.

MISO SYRUP

Makes: about 570ml (19fl oz)

Used in: Mi-So Happy, Vodka (page 106)

Ingredients: 500g (1lb) light or dark miso paste
1L (2pts) filtered water
2g (½tsp) methocellulose
1kg (2¼lb) caster (superfine) sugar

Note you will need a Thermomix for this recipe.

Make a soup by blending the miso paste and water in a Thermomix blender at 60°C (140°F). Leave to cool. Mix the methocellulose with 50g (2oz) of the soup mixture to make a paste. Add the remaining soup mix and put all the liquid back into the Thermomix.

Bring back up to 70°C (158°F) gently and a raft will form on the top. Remove the raft and you will be left with clear miso. Collect 1L (2pts) of clear miso and add it, together with the sugar to the Thermomix and stir for 15 minutes or until the sugar has dissolved. Bottle the syrup.

COCONUT SYRUP

Makes: 750ml (1½pts)

Used in: Bottle #1 Tomato, Vodka (page 126)

Ingredients:
500ml (1pt) raw coconut water (I use Chi)
500g (1lb) caster (superfine) sugar

Blend the ingredients in a blender on a medium speed until combined. Bottle the syrup.

CARAMEL SYRUP

Makes: about 500ml (1pt)

Used in: Parsnip, Whisky + Bourbon (page 152)

Ingredients:
500g (1lb) caster (superfine) sugar
525ml (1pt) water
cider vinegar

Put the sugar into a medium saucepan with 25ml (¾fl oz) of the water and a splash of vinegar (this helps prevent it from crystallizing). Heat gently over a medium heat until dark golden in colour. Pour onto a baking tray (sheet) and leave to cool and set.

Once set, smash up the sugar and put it into a heavy-duty blender and blend to a powder. Add the rest of the measured water and blend to make a syrup. Bottle.

MANGO SYRUP

Makes: 750ml (1½pts)

Used in: Mi-So Happy, Vodka (page 106)

Ingredients:
500ml (1pt) mango juice
500g (1lb) caster (superfine) sugar

Blend the ingredients in a blender on a medium speed until the sugar has dissolved. Strain using a superbag then bottle.

GINGER SYRUP

Makes: about 500ml (1pt)

Used in: Bangkok Penicillin, Vodka (page110)

Ingredients:
2kg (4¼lb) fresh ginger
caster (superfine) sugar

Juice the ginger. Weigh the liquid and add an equal amount of sugar to it. Place in a heavy-duty blender and blend until the sugar has dissolved. Bottle the syrup.

SOUR TOMATO SYRUP

Makes: 500ml (1pt)

Used in: Bottle #1 Tomato, Vodka (page 126)

Ingredients:
1kg (2¼lb) tomatoes
citric acid
malic acid

Juice the tomatoes. Distribute the juice evenly between the centrifuge buckets of your machine and spin at 4000 rpm for 20 minutes.

Pour the mixture into a measuring jug. For every 94ml (3fl oz) of juice you will need to add 4g (1tsp) of citric acid and 2g (½tsp) of malic acid. Stir until dissolved. Keep in the fridge and use within two weeks.

FERMENTED CUCUMBER SYRUP

Makes: 500ml (1pt)

Used in: Rök House Bellini, Gin (page 98)

Ingredients:
6 cucumbers, finely sliced using a mandolin
sea salt
caster (superfine) sugar

Weigh the sliced cucumber then add a quantity of sea salt in a 1% ratio to cucumber. Place both ingredients in a vac bag and seal it to the maximum without spillage.

Date the bag and store it in a dark place for approximately 1 month. Check the bag weekly until the mixture has turned to complete liquid. Strain the mixture using a chinois and collect the liquid in a glass bowl. Weigh the liquid and add it to a heavy-duty blender together with an equal part of sugar. Blend on a medium speed until completely combined. Strain, then bottle the syrup.

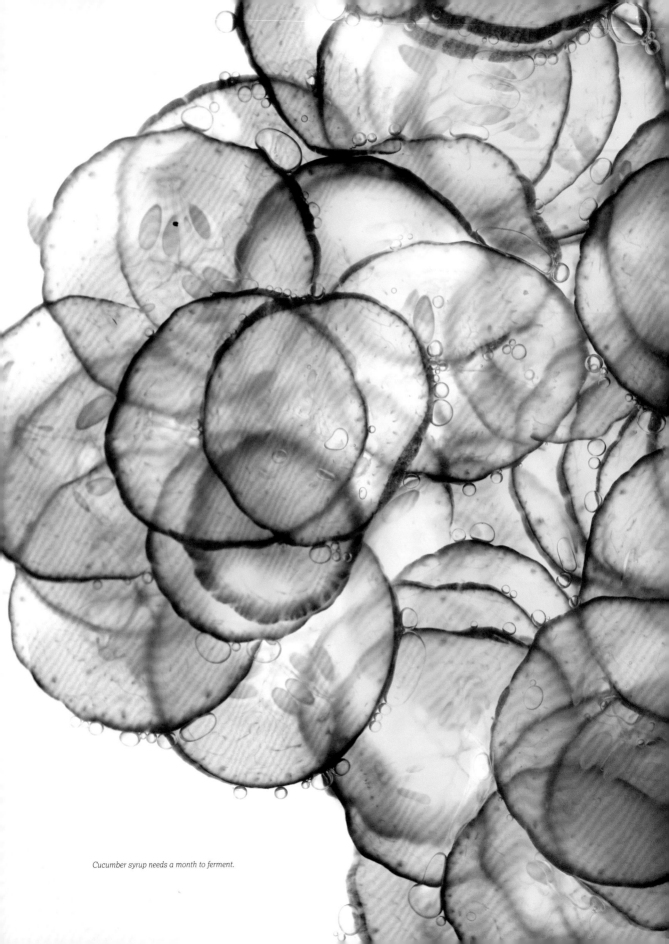

Cucumber syrup needs a month to ferment.

LIQUEURS

Liqueurs bridge the gap between a syrup and a spirit. They generally have a lower ABV than a spirit, and are delicious and simple to make so they're a good place to start when you're getting into cocktail making.

ROWAN BERRY LIQUEUR

Makes: about 1L (2pts)

Used in: Foraged Negroni, Wine + Vermouth (page 174)

Ingredients:

250g (9oz) rowan berries
750ml (1½pts) vodka
caster (superfine) sugar

Firstly, always buy rowan berries from your forager or farm shop when in season, and try to make enough liqueur to last the year.

Blitz the fruit in a blender then place the fruit and vodka in a large vac bag and seal to maximum pressure without spillage.

Set the water bath of a sous vide machine to 70°C (158°F), cook and leave to infuse for about 20 hours.

Strain the mixture using a chinois and collect the liquid in a large measuring jug. Add sugar in a ratio of 5g (1tsp) per 100ml (3½fl oz) and stir by hand until the sugar has dissolved. Strain and bottle.

Foraged Negroni

SMOKED PEACH LIQUEUR

Makes: about 750ml (1½pts)

Used in: Smoked Peach Bellini, Wine + Vermouth (page 166)

Ingredients:
500g (1lb) peaches
1ml (¼tsp) pectinase
vodka
caster (superfine) sugar

Cut the peaches in half and remove the stones. Set up your smoker and smoke the peach halves (see method on page 201) for about 20 minutes (you can smoke them a little longer if not using this liqueur for the bellini).

Leave to cool, then blend in a heavy-duty blender with the pectinase.

Divide the liquid evenly between the centrifuge buckets of your machine and spin at 4000 rpm for 20 minutes.

Pour off the mixture and measure the juice. Add an equal part of vodka to the peach juice. Measure this liquid and add 10g (2tsp) of sugar per 100ml (3½fl oz) of liquid. Stir until dissolved.

GRAPEFRUIT LIQUEUR

Makes: about 750ml (1½pts)

Used in: Lack of Faith, Tequila (page 184)

Ingredients:
3 grapefruit, peel only
700ml (1½pts) vodka
140g (5oz) caster (superfine) sugar

Infuse the grapefruit peel in the vodka for 1 week. Strain, then add 10g (2tsp) of sugar per 100ml (3½fl oz) of liquid. Stir until dissolved.

CLEMENTINE LIQUEUR

Makes: about 800ml (1¾pts)

Used in: Birds, Wine + Vermouth (page 170)

Ingredients:
350ml (12fl oz) clementine juice
350ml (12fl oz) vodka
150g (5½oz) caster (superfine) sugar

Combine the juice and vodka then stir in the sugar until dissolved. Bottle.

SODAS, JUICES + INFUSIONS

Making sodas and infusions is really simple. By following the principles in the recipes on this page you could try infusing and making sodas from almost anything you like.

CLARIFIED SPICED TOMATO

Makes: 1L (2pts)

Used in: TMF Bloody Mary, Vodka (page 116)

Ingredients:
1kg (2¼lb) cherry tomatoes
5g (1tsp) Maldon sea salt
1 large pinch celery salt
10ml (2tsp) Tabasco sauce
20g (⅔oz) Worcestershire sauce
1ml (¼tsp) pectinase

Blend all the ingredients in a heavy-duty blender on a medium speed for 5 minutes.

Divide the mixture evenly between the centrifuge buckets of your machine and spin at 4000 rpm for 30 minutes. Pour off the liquid and seal in a vac bag, removing all the air.

LEMON VERBENA INFUSION

Makes: 700ml (1½pts)

Used in: Thomas Wolsey, Wine + Vermouth (page 168)

Ingredients:
40g (1½oz) lemon verbena
1.5L (3pts) water

Add both ingredients to a small vac bag and seal to the maximum allowed without spillage. Place in the fridge and leave to infuse for 1 hour. Strain and bottle.

LEMON BALM SODA

Makes: about 1.5L (3pts)

Used in: Apple, Vodka (page 118)

Ingredients:
40g (1½oz) lemon balm
1.5L (3pts) water

Add both ingredients to a large vac bag and seal to the maximum allowed without spillage. Place in a fridge and leave to infuse for 4 hours. Strain and bottle. If not using in the Apple cocktail, this will need to be carbonated. If using in the Apple cocktail, the whole drink will be carbonated so there's no need to do it at this point.

Lemon verbena.

EGG SHELL SODA

Makes: 770ml (1⅔pts) soda

Used in: The Colour Blue, Gin (page 92)

Ingredients:
18 egg shells
70ml (2½fl oz) cider vinegar
300ml (10fl oz) filtered water

Remove the film from the egg shells and put the shells into a saucepan. Cover with water and bring to the boil to kill any bacteria. Simmer for 5 minutes then drain.

Preheat the oven to 180°C/350°F/Gas Mark 4. Put the egg shells into a roasting tin (pan) and roast for 5 minutes. Remove and set aside to cool.

Once cool, place in a heavy-duty blender and blend to a powder. Transfer the powder to a soda bottle with a tight seal, add the cider vinegar and water and seal the bottle immediately.

Leave the bottles for 3–4 days, or until the egg shell has dissolved. The reaction during the dissolving process should give off a by-product of carbon dioxide, thereby carbonating the liquid.

DISTILLATES

Distilling spirits is a way of adding a lot of flavour to something without adding anything else – they have very clean flavours – and are also a way of adding a taste you don't usually associate with drinks. That said, distillation is definitely something that requires trial and error. Once you've distilled something and have taken out the bitterness, salt, sugar etc., the flavour changes dramatically so I'm very regularly surprised by the results. Often you're just left with something that's got a lot of aroma without much flavour at all.

Distilling is the means by which I do most of my experimenting. It enables me to play with flavours and try different things.

At home, the safest and best way to distil is with a rotary evaporator. I do appreciate they are a very expensive piece of kit and are for keen enthusiasts, but for me they really are the only way to distil things and are something to invest in if you want to get serious about drinks. Even though I know that many of you won't be able to make these recipes yet, they are here to inspire you – perhaps to try making an infusion of one of them instead – and to make you think about different flavour combinations.

SALT BEEF DISTILLATE

Makes: about 600ml (1¼pts)

Used in: Groner Sazerac, Cognac (page 186)

Ingredients:
4 salt beef bagels with mustard pickles
1L (2pts) vodka

Place the salt beef bagels in a heavy-duty blender and blend until broken down into a thick mush. Transfer the blended bagels and vodka to a vac bag and seal. Leave to infuse overnight.

Pour the liquid into the evaporation flask of a rotary evaporator. Set the water bath to 60°C (140°F) and lower the pressure until all the liquid has evaporated. Measure the ABV and cut to 40% with filtered water (see page 83) then bottle.

HOP DISTILLATE

Makes: about 1L (2pts)

Used in: E2PA, Whisky + Bourbon (page 142)

Ingredients: 500ml (1pt) vodka; 25g (¾oz) Mosaic hops; 7g (¼oz) Cascade hops; 6g (⅕oz) Bravo hops; 2.5g (½tsp) Amarillo hops

Place all the ingredients in a vac bag and seal to the maximum pressure the bag will take without leaking. Infuse overnight. Strain through a chinois, pushing down to extract as much of the liquid as possible from the hops. Pour the liquid into the evaporation flask of a rotary evaporator. Set the water bath to 60°C (140°F) and lower the pressure until all the liquid has evaporated. Measure the ABV and cut to 40% with filtered water (see page 83) then bottle.

Groner Sazerac

CUSTARD DISTILLATE

Makes: 850ml (1¾pts)

Used in: Rhubarb, Vodka (page 138)

Ingredients:
750ml (1½pts) custard (made from a powder)
750ml (1½pts) vodka

Pour the liquid into the evaporation flask of a rotary evaporator. Set the water bath to 60°C (140°F) and lower the pressure until all the liquid has evaporated. Measure the ABV and cut to 40% with filtered water (see page 83) then bottle.

RICOTTA DISTILLATE

Makes: about 1L (2pts)

Used in: Thomas Wolsey, Wine + Vermouth (page 168)

Ingredients:
750g (1lb 10½oz) ricotta
750ml (1½pts) vodka

Add all the ingredients to a vac bag and seal to the maximum pressure without spillage. Leave to infuse overnight.

Divide the mixture equally between the centrifuge buckets of your machine and spin at 4000 rpm for 20 minutes. Pour off the liquid – there should be 1L (2pts).

Pour the liquid into the evaporation flask of a rotary evaporator. Set the water bath to 60°C (140°F) and lower the pressure until all the liquid has evaporated. Measure the ABV and cut to 40% with filtered water (see page 83) then bottle.

LEMON DISTILLATE

Makes: 300ml (10fl oz)

Ingredients:
rind of 6 lemons
300ml (10fl oz) vodka

Finely chop all the lemon rind. Place in a vac bag along with the vodka and seal to the maximum without spillage. Leave to infuse for 3 days.

Pour the liquid into the evaporation flask of a rotary evaporator. Set the water bath to 55°C (131°F) and lower the pressure until all the liquid has evaporated. Measure the ABV and cut to 40% with filtered water (see page 83) then bottle.

PARSLEY DISTILLATE

Makes: about 1L (2pts)

Used in: Bottle #2 Banana, Sake, (page 192)

Ingredients:
500g (1lb) flat leaf parsley
1L (2 pts) vodka

Blend the ingredients in a blender and place in a vac bag. Leave to infuse for 24 hours.

Pour the liquid into the evaporation flask of a rotary evaporator. Set the water bath to 50°C (122°F) and lower the pressure until all the liquid has evaporated. Measure the ABV and cut to 40% with filtered water (see page 83) then bottle.

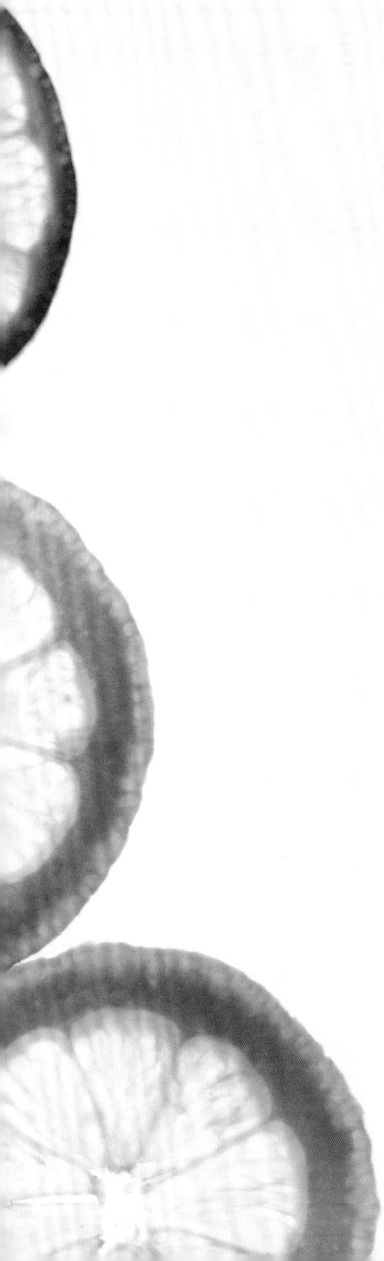

Hemp seeds.

PEA SHOOT DISTILLATE

Makes: 700ml (1½pts)

Used in: Pea Wine, Vermouth & Wine (page 160)

Ingredients:
250g (9oz) pea shoots
700ml (1½pts) vodka
100ml (3½fl oz) filtered water

Add the ingredients to a large vac bag and seal it to the maximum pressure without spillage. Leave at room temperature for 4 hours to infuse.

Strain and pour into the evaporation flask of a rotary evaporator. Set the water bath to 50°C (122°F) and lower the pressure until all the liquid has evaporated. Measure the ABV and cut to 40% with filtered water (see page 83) then bottle.

WHITEBEAM DISTILLATE

Makes: 700ml (½pts)

Used in: Cherry Bark, Vodka (page 132)

Ingredients:
50g (2oz) dried whitebeam berries
700ml (1½pts) vodka

Preheat your oven on its lowest setting. Blend the berries in a blender to break them up, then transfer them to a baking tray (sheet) and bake in the low oven for 8–10 hours (or dehydrate them in a dehydrator).

Transfer to the evaporation flask of a rotary evaporator along with the vodka. Set the water bath to 55°C (131°F) and lower the pressure until all the liquid has evaporated. Measure the ABV and cut to 40% with filtered water (see page 83) then bottle.

PRETZEL AND PEANUT BUTTER DISTILLATE

Makes: 500ml (1pt)

Used in: Pretzel Manger, Cognac (page 188)

Ingredients:
200g (7oz) peanut butter (crunchy or smooth)
750ml (1½pts) vodka
125g (4½oz) pretzels

Place all the ingredients in the evaporation flask of a rotary evaporator. Set the water bath to 50°C (122°F) and lower the pressure until all the liquid has evaporated. Measure the ABV and cut to 40% with filtered water (see page 83) then bottle.

SEAWEED DISTILLATE

Makes: 350ml (12fl oz)

Used in: The Colour Blue, Gin (page 92); Bastardized Gin Martini, Gin (page 102)

Ingredients:
250g (9oz) wakame (edible seaweed)
700ml (1½pts) vodka

Place the wakame and vodka in a vac bag and seal. Set the water bath of a sous vide machine to 55°C (131°F). Once at temperature, add the vac bag and leave for 45 minutes, then strain.

Pour the liquid into the evaporation flask of a rotary evaporator. Set the water bath to 55°C (131°F) and lower the pressure until all the liquid has evaporated. Measure the ABV and cut to 40% with filtered water (see page 83) then bottle.

AROMATIC THAI DISTILLATE

Makes: 1L (2pts)

Used in: Bangkok Penicillin, Vodka (page 110)

Ingredients:
1 red (bell) pepper, roughly chopped
2 spring onions (scallions), roughly chopped
100g (3½oz) button mushrooms, roughly chopped
30ml (1fl oz) oyster sauce
10g (⅓oz) red Thai chilli paste
60g (2oz) coriander (cilantro)
pinch of salt
pinch of black pepper
1L (2pts) vodka

Place the pepper, spring onions (scallions) and mushrooms in a heavy-duty blender and blend until smooth. Transfer the vegetables to a vac bag along with the remaining ingredients. Seal and leave to infuse overnight. Place all the ingredients in the evaporation flask of a rotary evaporator. Set the water bath to 55°C (131°F) and lower the pressure until all the liquid has evaporated. Measure the ABV and cut to 40% with filtered water (see page 83) then bottle.

HEMP SEED DISTILLATE

Makes: 500ml (1pt)

Used in: Carrot, Vodka (page 128)

Ingredients: 50g (2oz) hemp seeds; 500ml (1pt) vodka

Blend the hemps seeds in a heavy-duty blender to break up the shells. Place in the evaporation flask of a rotary evaporator along with the vodka. Set the water bath to 50°C (122°F) and lower the pressure until all the liquid has evaporated. Measure the ABV and cut to 40% (see page 83), then bottle.

SUPPLIERS

USEFUL ADDRESSES

BUCHI

this where I buy my Rotary Evaporators.

https://www.buchi.com/gb-en

HOP AND GRAPE

has great fermenting equipment; I buy the Essencia brand.

www.hopandgrape.co.uk

LAKELAND

has a great range of accessibly priced equipment, such as sous vide and vacuum packing machines aimed at the novice.

www.lakeland.co.uk

THE MALT MILLERS

for all brewing equipment, hops and malt

www.themaltmiller.co.uk

MASTER OF MALT

has an extensive range of spirits and they carry small samples so that you can try before you buy a large bottle.

www.masterofmalt.com

ODDBINS

has a good selection of spirits.

www.oddbins.com

SOUS CHEF

has a range of good-quality bar equipment as well as the smoker that I use (a Camerons Gourmet Mini Smoker) and the wood chips.

www.souschef.co.uk

SOUS VIDE TOOLS

has a good range of culinary equipment.

www.sousvidetools.com

SPECIAL INGREDIENTS

stocks items like Pectinex, as well as a variety of wood chips for a smoker.

www.specialingredients.co.uk

WESTLANDS

grows micro leaves, edible flowers, sea vegetables and unusual herbs such as apple marigold.

www.westlandswow.co.uk

WHISKY EXCHANGE

stocks nearly 3,500 different whiskies.

www.thewhiskyexchange.com

INDEX

ACKNOWLEDGMENTS

Firstly I would like to thank my wife Lucy, my 'innovation consultant' and my number one fan: you give me unwavering support and your creativity and passion inspire me to be better every day. You make me the person I am today and I love you.

My co-writer Imogen Fortes, you absolute super star; thank you for your patience, focus and passion.

My publisher Jacqui Small, editor Jo Copestick, and the whole team at Jacqui Small; thank you for your support and love for this project.

Richard Jung, your images are incredible; thanks for sharing the vision.

Thank you to all the chefs who continue to inspire me every day:

Tom Harris (One Leicester Street): thank you for the fridge raids and for believing in me.

Tom Sellers (Restaurant Story): for the freedom you have given me to burn bright and be creative.

Simon Rogan and Dan Cox (Fera): you opened my eyes to British produce and changed the way I think about ingredients.

Lee Westcott (Typing Room): my partner in crime at the Town Hall Hotel; thank you for being my chief taster!

Michael O' Hare (Rabbit in the Moon and The Man Behind the Curtain): I am truly honoured to work with you; thank you for allowing me never to shake cocktails.

And lastly to my team, my kids from Talented Mr Fox, Peg + Patriot and Scout: thank you for sharing the daily vision; your creativity, passion and determination have made this possible – you guys rock my world! Love Dad x

James, Ally, Sam, John, Ross, Aiden, Constanca, Hamish, Mark, Natalia, Alan, Will, Josh, Charles.

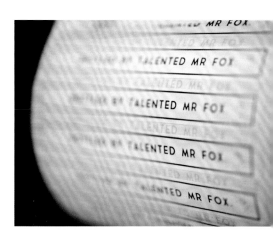